I0417164

Editor-in-Chief and Founder:
 Lyndon H. LaRouche, Jr.
Editorial Board: *Lyndon H. LaRouche, Jr. , Helga
 Zepp-LaRouche, Paul Gallagher, Tony Papert,
 Gerald Rose, Dennis Small, Jeffrey Steinberg,
 William Wertz*
Co-Editors: *Paul Gallagher, Tony Papert*
Managing Editor: *Nancy Spannaus*
Technology: *Marsha Freeman*
Books: *Katherine Notley*
Ebooks: *Richard Burden*
Graphics: *Alan Yue*
Photos: *Stuart Lewis*
Circulation Manager: *Stanley Ezrol*

INTELLIGENCE DIRECTORS
Counterintelligence: *Jeffrey Steinberg, Michele
 Steinberg*
Economics: *John Hoefle, Marcia Merry Baker,
 Paul Gallagher*
History: *Anton Chaitkin*
Ibero-America: *Dennis Small*
Russia and Eastern Europe: *Rachel Douglas*
United States: *Debra Freeman*

INTERNATIONAL BUREAUS
Bogotá: *Miriam Redondo*
Berlin: *Rainer Apel*
Copenhagen: *Tom Gillesberg*
Houston: *Harley Schlanger*
Lima: *Sara Madueño*
Melbourne: *Robert Barwick*
Mexico City: *Gerardo Castilleja Chávez*
New Delhi: *Ramtanu Maitra*
Paris: *Christine Bierre*
Stockholm: *Ulf Sandmark*
United Nations, N.Y.C.: *Leni Rubinstein*
Washington, D.C.: *William Jones*
Wiesbaden: *Göran Haglund*

ON THE WEB
e-mail: eirns@larouchepub.com
www.larouchepub.com
www.executiveintelligencereview.com
www.larouchepub.com/eiw
Webmaster: *John Sigerson*
Assistant Webmaster: *George Hollis*
Editor, Arabic-language edition: *Hussein Askary*

EIR (ISSN 0273-6314) *is published weekly
(50 issues), by EIR News Service, Inc.,
P.O. Box 17390, Washington, D.C. 20041-0390.
(703) 777-9451*

European Headquarters: E.I.R. GmbH, Postfach
Bahnstrasse 9a, D-65205, Wiesbaden, Germany
Tel: 49-611-73650
Homepage: http://www.eirna.com
e-mail: eirna@eirna.com
Director: Georg Neudecker

Montreal, Canada: 514-461-1557

Denmark: EIR - Danmark, Sankt Knuds Vej 11,
basement left, DK-1903 Frederiksberg, Denmark.
Tel.: +45 35 43 60 40, Fax: +45 35 43 87 57. e-mail:
eirdk@hotmail.com.

Mexico City: EIR, Sor Juana Inés de la Cruz 242-2
Col. Agricultura C.P. 11360
Delegación M. Hidalgo, México D.F.
Tel. (5525) 5318-2301
eirmexico@gmail.com

Canada Post Publication Sales Agreement
#40683579

Postmaster: Send all address changes to *EIR*, P.O.
Box 17390, Washington, D.C. 20041-0390.

Signed articles in *EIR* represent the views of the
authors, and not necessarily those of the Editorial
Board.

End-Game Against
The British Monarchy

A Mission Statement

May 21—Lyndon H. LaRouche, Jr., had arrived in India with a group of U.S. forces, when word arrived in April 1945, that President Franklin Roosevelt had died. A group of soldiers asked to have an evening meeting with LaRouche. He simply told them: the President is dead, and we have to, ourselves, all the more, assemble ourselves, and devote ourselves to the mission of President Roosevelt.

That was the beginning of Lyndon LaRouche's mission, now almost exactly seventy years old, which still today is not over,—although it has now come to a critical fork in the road over the past roughly two weeks.

"We were coming towards the end of the actual conflict in Europe, and then beyond," LaRouche remembered today. "And so, what I was left with, was the Southeast Asia area. I got more or less tied to that region, plus Russia. And what I otherwise had gotten into."

LaRouche wrote to General Dwight Eisenhower in 1948, asking him to run for President, which would have denied the wretched Harry Truman a second term, and replaced him with someone who aspired to what Franklin Roosevelt had represented. At that time, Eisenhower was being brought in as the new president of Columbia University in New York. "Eisenhower was the one person I had access to," LaRouche said today. "He was then going into his position at Columbia; that was my access to him."

We now know that all four of Franklin Roosevelt's surviving sons, were themselves also writing just such letters to Eisenhower at the same time. Nevertheless, he waited out Truman's term before running, and winning, in 1952.

What some regard as LaRouche's excursion into the socialist movement during the 1950s and early 1960s, was actually much more specific. He supported and then joined the Socialist Workers Party, an American Trotskyist party, because it was fighting McCarthyism (better called Trumanism), as LaRouche was also doing on his own. No other such national organization was doing this, including the Communist Party.

The High Point

Later, LaRouche intervened into the "New Left," such as the Students for a Democratic Society, in the interests of bringing forth something productive in the wake of the 1963 assassination of President John F. Kennedy. "My commitment was very, very clear," he remembered today, "but the times were changing. And therefore, the things that you dealt with at an earlier time, no longer fit the situation."

His crushing defeat of the leading British Keynesian Abba Lerner in a Queens College debate in 1971, pre-

EIRNS/Stuart Lewis

LaRouche and Reagan at a National Rifle Association Presidential candidates event in Concord, N.H., February 1980

vented a British takeover of the U.S. and its economy at that time. "It was the birth of the time when people began to congeal themselves around me," LaRouche said today. "It was an easy fight for me; Abba Lerner was just a damn fool. A self-important damn fool. But the whole crew of Keynesians was really freaked out at the fact that I had defeated them."

LaRouche's Strategic Defense Initiative (SDI) proposal of 1977 and thereafter, was publicly adopted by President Reagan, and also unofficially supported by the then-existing Russian government, nominally under Leonid Brezhnev. This was the highest point of success ever achieved to that point, of LaRouche's mission to reshape the U.S. Presidency to that which Alexander

Hamilton had originally intended, which included what later President John Quincy Adams had termed a "community of principle" among republican nations girdling the globe. Not only did the SDI include an agreement between the U.S. and the Soviets for development of devices based on "new physical principles" to overcome thermonuclear missiles. It also included the joint U.S.-Soviet use of these technologies for economic development of Africa, Asia, and Ibero-America.

President Reagan suffered an assassination attempt by Bush-linked forces, two months after his inauguration. Although he survived, he was severely wounded, and he loosened or dropped the reins of government, which were taken over by the Bush family, which killed the SDI and railroaded LaRouche to jail.

LaRouche's arrest (before his frameup trial and five-year incarceration in Federal prison), was actually intended to have been an assassination, which was only prevented by an intervention from the White House. The intention was also to kill LaRouche in prison, but patriotic forces kept him safe there.

EIRNS/Rachel Douglas

Lyndon and Helga LaRouche in Red Square, April 1994

Mission to Russia

The way LaRouche got to Russia, was that he got permission to go to Germany, to be with his wife Helga. And she had already adopted a course of action, which was the same as his.

"I was in Europe," he said today, "and then, in the process, because of Helga's Russian connections, I found myself flying into Moscow with Helga. I found myself parked there.

"At the special meeting with the leaders of Russia at that time, they asked me for my decision. What should they do? We agreed on that. Then, Bill Clinton did not oppose it,—in fact, he agreed with it, in principle. But he was not going to act so as to put me, directly, in front of this stuff. But Bill actually did do a lot, in order to coordinate his views with me.

"Also up to that point, we had a friend in the Papacy. That Pope was also wounded in an assassination attempt. What happened is, the other party, shall we say the radical, left-wing party of the clergy, took advantage of the fact that the Pope had an impairment in his functioning, and they came in like gang-busters. Therefore, the whole Catholic operation disintegrated, and, interestingly, the disintegration of the Catholic Church from that point on, meant that the whole Church kind of faded because of this kind of disintegration.

"The new Pope Francis is trying to make sure that that's not going to be repeated."

Out of the bankruptcy of Russia, which also involved the bankruptcy of the whole world financial system, LaRouche brought back a proposal of his from Russia, which was eventually adopted by President Clinton.

"I came back again," he said today, "at the same time that Putin was rising in power, and dealing with the Chechens. I was also without any direct connection to Putin at that time. I didn't really know him much, but I just knew about him. But the Chechen issue was the same issue I was working on. And that's the whole racket we're dealing with right now."

Clinton went with the proposal; then he was sexgated and impeached in a phony process.

"It was simply an operation done by a bunch of Republican whores on behalf of Queen Elizabeth II herself," LaRouche said today. "Agents of the Queen [like Ambrose Evans-Pritchard] directed and controlled the Republican Party. It's probably still true today. What you can say, is what's the difference between the Republican Party,—well, most of them are queens."

The hounding of Bill Clinton out of office entailed

Martin O'Malley, March 29, 2015

the loss of Glass-Steagall, followed by two terms of George W. Bush and almost two of Obama. It gave us a world economic catastrophe, and a series of U.S. wars of aggression, leaving us now on the brink of thermonuclear World War III.

In a Position To Win

Now, we're come back to where we were, only again it's different. But Obama can be out at any day of this week or next week; his crimes have been exposed, and he can't recover.

"He could not have won the so-called election, nor could he have maintained his influence in the United States now, except for the British monarchy," LaRouche says. "He's just the Queen's tool. You need to know what his gender is; because you look at the women that work around him,—you wonder what his gender is."

Now with O'Malley doing what he's doing, we're at the position where we can win the Presidency; the real American Presidency, as Lyndon LaRouche has been fighting for, for all these seventy years.

"There's a good way of looking at that," LaRouche said today, "because O'Malley had not, on a formal basis, had not seemed to be, what he has become now. But, really he hasn't changed. What happened is, is that he, like most politicians,—even good ones,—he will always try to wear the costume which fits the constituency. And that was the case with him, at an earlier stage.

"When he ran up against this Obama problem and what went with it, then, he un-masked himself, and what he did, was not something he had intended to do earlier; even though his actual feelings about the matter, had not been much different from what they are now.

But, it didn't show that way under the earlier conditions. Now, he gets to the point where he's at the period of his life where he's saying, 'Hey, I've got to get back into the fight here.'

"And that's exactly what has happened."

Another Mission Statement

by Tony Papert

May 22—Another way to pose the mission of this issue, is Lyndon LaRouche's pilgrimage to, and through the Twentieth Century, and into the Twenty-First.

I was always deeply moved by Jacob's answer to Pharaoh in Genesis, because it seemed to be the first mention of life as a "pilgrimage." On first meeting him, Pharaoh had asked Jacob how old he was.

And Jacob said unto Pharaoh, The days of the years of my pilgrimage are an hundred and thirty years: few and evil have the days of the years of my life been, and have not attained unto the days of the years of the life of my fathers in the days of their pilgrimage.

And I think it no coincidence that the foundation-stone of English literature was Chaucer's *Canterbury Tales*, in which all of the life of each one of us, from end to end, is seen as a pilgrimage. It begins in the spring of life, in "Aprille." It ends, God willing, in the *Winterreise*, whose final song was rendered by Frank Mathis in Lyn's *Musikabend* of May 10, summarized in *EIR* no. 21.

Lyndon LaRouche was not alone; he began this journey under the Presidency of Franklin Roosevelt; and he achieved notable success under the Presidency of Ronald Reagan.

Lyn's long pilgrimage intersected that of Bill Clinton. I understand that that whole story began when Lyn was in prison; it wound its way through his mission to Moscow, and then through Bill's victimization through a sex-scandal. And after more than twenty years, this long duet has still not yet ended,—the final words of the final chapter are still not yet written, as Pushkin and Mussorgsky portentously begin their opera *Boris Godunov*.

Lyn's long pilgrimage has intersected those of Presidents and Popes, great musicians, and generals and others who have spent their talent for the betterment and the salvation of mankind.

"Watchman, what of the night?"

EIR Contents

www.larouchepub.com Volume 42, Number 22, May 29, 2015

Cover This Week

Great Seal of the Realm

royal.gov.uk

End-Game Against The British Monarchy

by Benjamin Deniston

This is an edited version of Benjamin Deniston's contribution to the <u>LaRouche PAC webcast</u> of Friday, May 22, 2015.

May 22—I was in a discussion with Mr. LaRouche earlier in the week, and his response to [California Gov.] Jerry Brown's move to now suppress and make it more difficult to develop desalination, and his pursuit of these insane carbon emissions, was rather straightforward: "This guy's just a pathetic fool. He's a pathetic fool, and he's acting for people and on behalf of policies that go much beyond him." He is, in effect, absolutely acting to pursue and implement the policy of the British Royal Family, the policy of the British Empire, of population reduction, the stated, on-the-books, on-the-record policy of the Queen of England, of her Royal Consort Prince Philip, of their associates in the Anglo-Dutch establishment and their allies on Wall Street,—to reduce the world population by billions of people, potentially down to a level of one to two billion people. And Jerry Brown's policies, as he's shown, are clearly acting to be consistent with the implementation of that ideology, that program.

I think this desalination matter is just typical. Any sane, human government—like that of his father, for example, Pat Brown—what would his response be? He would have already accelerated the development of these desalination systems. You have systems that are being designed, being built, being constructed; others that have been mothballed, that are being examined again; he would have said, "Get these things going as quickly as possible!" You'd use the power of the authority of the state to accelerate the development of these new water supplies.

Jerry Brown does the exact opposite. He's suppressing them; he makes it more difficult. He's stopping the already-existing, relatively small-scale attempts to alleviate some of the drought conditions in these coastal regions. But again, this is an expression of his adherence to this genocidal, zero-growth, population-reduction policy, that actually has been developed and imple-

gov.ca.gov

California Gov. Jerry Brown issues his latest genocidal decree, in Sacramento May 19.

mented, and stated by the British Royal Family, by the British Empire and their associates.

So that's the real issue. That's what Jerry Brown is expressing right now. This is what we have to overcome. This is what we have to defeat: This is what we have to defeat in California, in the West, in the United States generally. And this is the expression, really, of a much deeper policy, a much deeper cultural issue for mankind, which is the fight against Zeus, this Zeusian ideology.

Zeus Against Humanity

We've discussed on this program—my associate Jason Ross has done a lot to elaborate—what we know about the story of the fight of Prometheus against Zeus. And you look at the insight we get into the long-standing history of mankind from these tales, from these stories, from these records. You look at the conditions of mankind under the reign of Zeus, as described by Aeschylus: You have mankind living in a state of bestiality,—no science, no technology, no art, no culture. These were the conditions that man was kept in by Zeus!

And when Prometheus freed mankind from these conditions, when Prometheus raised mankind to an ability to go beyond these animal-like conditions, to develop science, to develop art, to be human,—it was for *that*, that Zeus sought to destroy Prometheus, sought to punish him. That is what Zeus is.

And we see this in other accounts of Zeus. I was looking at some of the ancient Greek accounts of the Trojan War, in the *Cypria*, and I'd like to read one quote that gives you another insight into the quality of this Zeusian character. It reads:

There was a time when the countless tribes of men, though widespread, oppressed the surface of the deep-bosomed Earth. And Zeus saw this, and he had pity, and in his wise heart resolved to relieve the all-nurturing Earth of men, by causing the great struggle of the Trojan war, that the

Illustrated London News, December 22, 1849
Depiction of the Irish potato famine

load of death might empty the world. And so the heroes were slain in Troy, and the plan of Zeus came to pass.[1]

So again, from another record, another insight into the mentality of Zeus: to release loads of death upon mankind, to empty the Earth of the human population, to free Mother Nature of this burden of mankind. It might sound similar to some of what people say today.

These are ancient accounts from the depths of ancient Greece, but they're indications of the mentality, the cultural disease that has plagued mankind,—that mankind has had to fight against,—for a very, very long period of time. And today, we're seeing the most recent expression of this Zeusian ideology, this Zeusian force, which is the British Empire. This is the most recent expression, the British, or you could call it the Anglo-Dutch Empire,—the most recent expression of this Zeusian, oligarchical ideology: the use of famines to cause mass death and reduce populations. Look at what the British did in India, for centuries, literally killing millions of Indians, through a policy of famine, of mass starvation, of economic policies designed to wipe out huge sections of the Indian population.

They did the same thing in Ireland. In the so-called "Irish potato famine:" 25% of the population of Ireland either left out of desperation, or was starved to death, under the policies of the British Empire at the time, under the justification of the ideology of Thomas Malthus, as the expression of this mentality then.

British Royal Eugenicists

So you have this long-standing expression of this oligarchical, this Zeusian policy which has plagued mankind, plagued civilization for thousands of years, in various expressions, various ways,—the British Empire being the most recent. And the most recent expression

---

1. For more, see "War, the Oligarchy and the Ancient Myth of Overpopulation," by Theodore J. Andromidas, *EIR*, May 3, 2013.

of this policy in the British Empire, is the creation of the so-called environmentalist movement.

I want to take a few minutes just to put on the table a few facts. There's extensive material that we've pulled together, Mr. LaRouche and his organization have pulled together over the years, documenting this.

But this, I think, has to be put on the record now, to get a sense of what Jerry Brown is really just a tool of, and what has to be overturned, what has to be overthrown, if California is going to survive,—if the West is going to survive. So if you look at this past century, I'm going to highlight a couple of leading individual figures, of the British, or of the Anglo-Dutch establishment, and their role in the creation of the so-called environmentalist movement, initially the "conservation movement."

You had Julian Huxley, who was a leader of the eugenics movement, before World War II,—but then also after World War II, after we witnessed Hitler's implementation of a eugenics program, the horrors of the Hitler regime, Julian Huxley continued to promote the development of eugenics, famously writing in the founding document of UNESCO, that despite the political backlash and horrific response that has occurred since the documentation of what Hitler did, despite this tarnishing of the name of the eugenics, we still have to support eugenics, "so that much that now is *unthinkable* may at least become thinkable," to use his words; to ensure that the revival of eugenics is possible. And he proceeded to then become President of the British Eugenics Society from '59-'62. That's one individual.

You take another, Prince Bernhard of the Netherlands, who was a member of the Nazi Party, who was a member of Nazi intelligence. According to reports in the 1970s, published in *Newsweek* and other locations, testimony at the Nuremberg trials showed that Prince Bernhard was a part of a special Nazi SS intelligence unit, working at IG Farben, where the Nazis later devel-

UNESCO

Eugenicist, and "environmentalist" Julian Huxley

oped the concentration camps and the slave-labor system. That was before the war. He resigned from the Nazi Party to marry a Dutch princess, signing his resignation letter, "Heil Hitler," and then received congratulations from Hitler, written to him for his wedding.

But he didn't abandon his Nazi pedigree, because after the war, he took up the leadership of Royal Dutch Airlines at a period when Royal Dutch Airlines, for one reason or another, abandoned their normal policy of documenting all of the people they flew around, and flew a number of Nazi war criminals out of Germany, to other locations in the world, so that they could escape prosecution.

Then you have Prince Philip, the unfortunately still-living Royal Consort, married to the current Queen of England. He himself, through family connections, has very close ties to elements of the Nazis, and he has openly stated that he would love to be reincarnated as a deadly virus, to help with what he thinks is the biggest problem facing the world, which is overpopulation,—that there are too many people. He would love to return as a deadly virus to eliminate huge sections of the world population. This is a person who's openly quoted saying that he believes that human society should be subject to periodic "cullings," to rid the world of excess people.

'Environmentalist' Genocide

So these are three leading figures of this Anglo-Dutch establishment. And what do they have in common besides support of Nazis, and eugenics, and mass killing, based on these ideologies? These are the people that founded the modern environmentalist movement. They founded the World Wildlife Fund, as a leading organization in the creation of the environmentalist movement in '60s. They created the "1001 Club" to organize major financial support to get this movement off the ground, running and spreading its propaganda and policies around the world.

And what is the policy of these organizations, of the World Wildlife Fund, of these environmentalist groups? Mass reduction of the human population. Reduce the world population by billions, down to maybe one or two billion people. That is the stated, active policy of these organizations, expressing the most modern expressions of this Zeusian mass-kill ideology, this Zeusian mass-kill policy.

They've picked up and promoted the whole climate change fraud, as a leading excuse, a leading guise to push this population reduction program. To claim that your driving your car is going to destroy the entire planet,—so therefore, we need to enforce legally binding, international limitations on carbon emissions. Which is really to restrict growth, restrict the production of power, restrict industry, restrict population growth,—through these radical, environmentalist means, under the guise of climate change.

To the degree that fools like Obama say, "Denying climate change now is a potential threat to national security," when the planet hasn't even warmed in almost 18 years! The actual planetary temperature has flatlined for nearly two decades, and these guys want to claim that we're having some catastrophic affect that's going to destroy the planet, in some short period of time. It's just insanity at this point.

I think it's worth highlighting a recent expression of this. Look back six years, to one of the last major attempts to try to put into place a major international treaty, a legally binding agreement to force nations to reduce their carbon emissions,—the so-called Copenhagen Climate Summit in 2009. China and India, in alliance with other nations, stated that they were not going to go along with a legally binding treaty to force them to reduce their carbon dioxide emissions, and they even threatened to walk out of the summit if that was forced upon them. Now, when this was made public in the days and weeks preceding the 2009 summit, the Queen herself freaked out, and used her opportunity of addressing the gathering of the heads of the Commonwealth nations—although many are not really na-

World Wildlife Fund

Prince Philip wants you to give him a hand.

tions—the Commonwealth dominions of the British Empire, to insist that this was their number-one policy, to get this Copenhagen climate treaty through, to ensure that they implemented this carbon reduction policy.

So in her own words, as recently as 2009, she declared that the policy of the British Empire *is* this climate change policy, is this population reduction program coming out of these leading Nazis, eugenicists, etc.

So this is the reality of the matter; this is the policy that's on the books, that's active, and that Jerry Brown has signed onto. He says that we need to stop growth, stop development, and lower the population,—claiming that that's what we have to do; and when people take measures that show we don't have to do that, he tries to stop them from taking those measures,—not letting them develop the resources that could be developed to alleviate the conditions. He has fully bought into and is implementing what has already been designed and acted upon as a global depopulation policy. When he tries to organize for this insane reduction in carbon emissions, he has fully bought into this British Royal Family genocide program.

So the effects are going to be there, however conscious Jerry Brown may be of the full origins of this policy,—I don't know how much it even matters at this point. But the effects are going to be real. He's right now acting as a tool, in his actions, of these people and of these policies. And so the lives of the people of California, the lives of the people of the West, depend on getting Jerry Brown out of there, as Mr. LaRouche said earlier today. Get Obama out, you can have Jerry Brown go out with him.

The Water Is There!

And with that shift, we have the policies, we have the programs: We can address the water issue. I think it's a little bit ironic, and somewhat useful, that right now what's being claimed as the basis for reaching the end of growth, is the issue of water. When the entire planet is covered in water, they're saying that mankind has reached the limits of growth because we're running

The unfinished Huntington Beach, Calif. desalination plant

out of water! And then, some cities say, "Well, we can just pull that out of the oceans here." And Jerry Brown says, "No, no! You can't do that, we're not going to let you do that. We're out of water. You didn't hear what I said!" It's insane.

They're claiming that we're out of water, and that's the reason that we've reached the limit to growth, when in reality, this is one of the most easily accessible expressions for what natural resources really are for mankind: They're not self-defined; they're not finite; they're a function of mankind's capabilities! Maybe hundreds of years ago, with the ability we had at that time, sure, we couldn't support a population of tens of millions of people in California. Now we can support a larger population than that, because we can manage the water supplies we need, to ensure that the cyclical aspects of the water system are large enough and intense enough to support the population of California and the West at a growing and accelerating rate.

And as we've discussed, the frontier issue we have in dealing with this now, is the galactic perspective, the galactic principle. At the same time that these fools are saying we've reached the limits to growth, at exactly the same time, we're right now, in recent years, in recent decades, getting completely new insights into how what we thought were basic water systems, are being controlled by our galaxy! We're understanding that; we're actually understanding the role of our entire galactic system, as an active force shaping the conditions we experience on Earth.

That's an *awesome* thought, that mankind is doing that: We're conceptualizing this massive system, containing billions of stars like our Sun, operating as a massive, coherent structure, in ways we can't even explain today,—that we don't fully understand. But we can begin to get an insight into that structure, that system, how that subsumes the Earth, how that subsumes the climate and the water systems. We're now developing an understanding of that, but in a way that can allow us to manage those conditions, to manage how the atmospheric moisture behaves, so to speak. We're getting insights into how this galactic influence shapes and modulates the activity of atmospheric moisture. That's critical: Atmospheric moisture is the source of all water on land. All of our water supplies depend upon these atmospheric moisture flows. If we can begin to tap into methods of affecting those, controlling those, and managing those, you're providing a completely new perspective on the reality of the fact that there are no limits to growth for mankind.

So I think it's incredibly ironic that these degenerates, either genocidal individuals, or fools that buy into this propaganda of these genocidalists,—are saying that we're right now reaching the limits to growth; that California has to be depopulated; we have to stop the development of California, because we've reached the limit to water supplies,—at exactly the time we're looking at the potential to completely revolutionize how mankind understands his relationship to the planet Earth, from the standpoint of acting from a galactic perspective, a galactic standpoint.

So I think that defines the battle lines rather clearly, and I think it goes without saying, which side Prometheus would be on, at this point. It may not be fire we're having here—it's water. But I think he would be fully inclined to be supportive.

FDR's Mission: Our Future, as We Are Given the Ability To Know It

by Phil Rubenstein

History is full of seeming coincidences. Franklin Delano Roosevelt, thirty-third President of the United States, the only President to be elected to four terms, died on April 12, 1945 in Warm Springs, Georgia. His funeral and burial took place in Washington, D.C. and Hyde Park, N.Y., respectively. April fourteenth and fifteenth, seventy years to the day after the assassination and death of President Abraham Lincoln. The sixteenth President of the United States was murdered five days after General Lee's surrender at Appomattox, effectively ending the War of Southern Rebellion. FDR died less than one month before the defeat of Nazism in World War II. In both cases, they were succeeded by men who, if not traitors, were far too small-minded, too petty to carry the mission of their predecessors. In this way, was the mission of our nation, in the wake of these crises of Imperial destruction, imperiled even to this day.

As described elsewhere in this issue of *EIR*, as word spread of FDR's passing, young men, still at war, wondered what the future would be for them, their families, their nation, or, for some, humanity.

In some cases, these men knew, that that future was up to them and their understanding of FDR's mission as President of the United States—and even a deepening of that purpose.

One such case was the young Lyndon LaRouche in the Burma-China-India theater, where there was nearly half a year of war still ahead. He was asked by his comrades what to expect, and he understood then what was to be expected of him.

LaRouche ended his service in India as its struggle for Independence was being fought. India was a country that played a leading role in what FDR understood

President Franklin D. Roosevelt

his mission and that of his country, to be.

Roosevelt's conception of these purposes is the force which led this nation to overcome the Depression, defeat Fascism, and, by the end of the war, to stand on the brink, not only of ending Empire, especially the British Empire, but of a great leap toward fulfilling the American Revolution in the form of a new relation among independent nations, freed from colonialism to develop their own powers of human creativity.

Reviving Hamilton's Principle

Much of what is said or written about FDR, in its sheer banality, amounts to little but gossip, or more to the point, slander. He was not a clever pol, or a pragmatic maneuverer of policies and people, or merely a "first-rate temperament." Even the sympathetic portrayal of his battle with polio misses the point. His purpose was not simply to walk, or to get back to politics as it was; his purpose was to revive Hamiltonian economics and human value, and the Presidency itself, as the core principles of the United States. His conception of the General Welfare, the Forgotten Man, was deepened during his Presidency, as was his sense of the historic import of those purposes.

That his economic principles were those of Hamilton's conception of the development of labor as the basis of credit and value, is shown in his policies as governor of New York, which precisely foreshadowed the New Deal with old-age security and unemployment insurance, as well as infrastructure and electrification. It was the same outlook behind his assignment of Harry Hopkins to drive the Works Progress Administration (WPA), and then Lend-Lease. In each case, he rejected the monetarist standards through which the British had driven the world to disaster.

Even more conclusive is FDR's explicitly defining of the New Deal in terms of the Preamble to the Constitution to which, as recently demonstrated in Bob Ingraham's report, Hamilton and his allies formulated the Preamble to shape the Constitution around the General Welfare and "our posterity." In the introduction to Volume 2 of his Public Papers[1] he says:

The New Deal was fundamentally intended as a modern expression of ideals set forth 150 years ago in the Preamble of the Constitution of the United States 'a more perfect union, justice, tranquility, the common defense, the general welfare and the blessings of liberty to ourselves and our posterity.'

Roosevelt throughout was clear that Wall Street, the financial sector, the speculators, were the problem. As he famously said in the 1936 campaign, "They hate me and I welcome their hatred."

It was FDR's Hamiltonian revival that made the United States the industrial provider for Great Britain, the USSR, and others, as well as for the United States itself. From Lend-Lease to the U.S. entry into the war, it was U.S. industry and its ability to develop its Labor Power and its military personnel that fueled our decisive role in victory.

Creating a New Sense of Humanity

Winning the war was a mission that FDR enabled, but it was not the mission of the Presidency. That mission was about the future: the ability to create a world in which these wars did not occur.

FDR, as others, like General MacArthur and General Eisenhower, saw the hideous nature of World War II—the death, the brutality, the growing destructiveness of weaponry, the insanity—as a threat to humanity's existence. At the same time, solving that threat, meant a great leap to a new sense of humanity. FDR's Presidential mission was to make the Presidency of the United States of America a leader for that future.

Among the clear signs of this, little noted today, was his fierce opposition to his strange ally Winston Churchill, on the continuance of British Imperial rule. The case of India makes the point. For FDR, the war was to end the colonialism and imperial policy that caused the war. We were not fighting to maintain

---

1. *The Public Papers and Addresses of Franklin D. Roosevelt*, Vol. 2.

Empire. India should gain its independence, even during the war. Churchill was apoplectic, as FDR made numerous suggestions as to how to accomplish that independence. For FDR, independence was never separated from economic development.

In the case of China, Roosevelt recognized its potential greatness and its past greatness, and insisted on its inclusion in the Big Four. The British, in the person of Churchill, denigrated the Chinese, and only reluctantly agreed to recognize them as a part of the Alliance, meanwhile undercutting them at every chance.

And of course, it was Roosevelt who drew the Soviet Union into the Dialogue of Nations, knowing full well, that this was crucial to winning the war, and the future. Churchill, Wall Street, and the likes of Lord Bertrand Russell wanted the United States to use the atomic bomb to force the Soviets to capitulate to Western financial and political hegemony. Much more could be said on this.

FDR's Mission was to use the Presidency to lead a dialogue of independent nations, able to solve problems from a common base of mutual development, with open and shared science and technology. He knew this was the only alternative to self-destruction. He himself had reversed the destruction led by two rabidly anglophile, pro-confederate Presidents of the United States: Woodrow Wilson and Theodore Roosevelt. The rule of slavery had to be ended globally.

FDR knew the unique capacity of the Hamiltonian Presidency. He not only fought Wall Street and the Judiciary, and the State's Rights mask of the pro-British Confederacy, but he used the Presidency to define a common mission for a united nation.

So today, Lyndon LaRouche revives the Presidency destroyed by the Bushes, Cheney, and Obama by invoking the same Alexander Hamilton, centered in the same New York from which Roosevelt acted. Now a global development movement exists, led by China, India, and Russia, exactly as foreseen by Roosevelt, countries whose policies and ideas have been inspired by Lyndon and Helga LaRouche and their recognition of the true nature of humanity, as Roosevelt did in his mission.

We are building the World Land-Bridge; we need now the very relations among nations that FDR had foreseen in his view of the post-war world. Seventy years later, as we can explore the astrophysical and use the micro-physical, we can create the future—that was his mission.

The Mission of Robert Kennedy

by Donald Phau

May 25—The assassination of President John F. Kennedy, and the coverup of the British-sponsored conspiracy which accomplished it, marked a decisive downward turning point for the United States, from which our country has not yet recovered. The patriotic tradition of FDR, which dictated assertive Federal government action for the General Welfare at home, and cooperation for global economic development abroad, appeared to be all but buried.

But, could the British oligarchical enemies of the United States be sure that JFK's anti-imperialist tradition was gone for good?

One major problem for their plans was on the horizon. Less than one year after Jack's murder, Robert F. Kennedy, the President's brother and Attorney General, left his position in the Johnson administration, and announced his candidacy for the Democratic Senatorial nomination from New York. Few knowledgeable politicians doubted at that time, that he was on his way to a run for the Presidency, and in a good position to win.

As President, Robert Kennedy would have ended United States-led Viet Nam war and taken up the Franklin Roosevelt programs of his brother, to revitalize the U.S. economy. This is the context in which to see the assassination of Robert Kennedy in June 1968, on the evening of his victory in the Democratic Presidential Primary in California.[1]

Robert Kennedy, with his brother President John Kennedy, at the White House Rose Garden.

With RFK out of the way, Richard Nixon won the 1968 Presidential race, paving the pathway for future devastation of the nation by the British and the Bushes. As President, Nixon promoted then-Congressman George H.W. Bush, to lead key committees in Congress, and in 1973 asked Bush to head the Republican National Committee. The murder of RFK could be said to have been a stepping stone to the rise of the traitorous Bushes, and their successor-in-crime Barack Obama.

Why was RFK a threat to the British Empire?

Kennedy's Fight for Civil Rights

When Jack Kennedy was elected President in 1960, Robert became his Attorney General, and was thus thrust into the center of the intense conflicts which dominated Kennedy's short administration—including civil rights on the domestic front, and potential thermonuclear confrontation with the Soviet Union on the international scene.

While intensively involved in the Administration's

---

1. The fact that the convicted assassin of RFK, Sirhan Sirhan, could not have been the sole killer has been raised continually, through analysis of the number of gunshots fired, the direction from which the fatal shot came, and the like. Most damning was the fact that Sirhan Sirhan stood in front of RFK with his pointed gun, but the Los Angeles coroner, Thomas Noguchi, ruled that the fatal bullet came from behind Kennedy.

attempts to calm racial tensions at home, RFK also became involved in racial politics by making a trip to South Africa in 1961. Although Prime Minister Hendrik Verwoerd refused to meet him, he went to Cape Town and was met by three thousand people when his plane landed. At the University of Cape Town he said:

> Few have the greatness to bend history itself, but each of us can work to change a small portion of events, and in the total of all those acts will be written the history of this generation. ... It is from numberless acts of courage and belief such as these that human history is shaped. Each time a man stands up for an ideal, or acts to improve the lot of others, or strikes out against injustice, he sends forth a tiny ripple of hope, and crossing each other from a million different centers of energy and daring, those ripples build a current which can sweep down the mightiest walls of oppression and resistance.

Finding Solace in the Greek Classics

It is impossible to overemphasize the turning point which occurred in Robert Kennedy's life and thinking due to the assassination of his brother. After that trauma, he found his primary solace in the Greek classics. RFK's Senate staff said he knew the Greeks cold. "He would cite some play, and say, 'You know that?' We didn't at all."

Historian Arthur Schlesinger writes in *Robert Kennedy and His Times*, that a year after JFK's assassination, Jacqueline Kennedy gave Robert Edith Hamilton's book *The Greek Way*. RFK proceeded to immerse himself in the writings of the ancient Greeks. One verse he memorized and cited often was from *Agamemnon* by Aeschylus:

> He who learns must suffer. And even in our sleep pain that cannot forget, falls drop by drop upon the heart, and in our despair, against our will, comes wisdom to us by the awful grace of God.
> [This would be written on his tombstone-ed.]

At gatherings of friends he would often recite a passage from Sophocles:

> The long days store up many things nearer to grief than joy
> Death at the last, the deliverer.
> Not to be born is past all prizing best.
> Next best by far when one has seen the light
> Is to go thither swiftly whence he came.

By the summer of 1964, Robert Kennedy had determined that he himself had to take up the mantle of his brother. He quit the Attorney Generalship, and in August began his campaign for Senator from New York State, an action which drew enormous ire from the whole left liberal establishment. Such stellar liberals as Gore Vidal, I.F. Stone, Paul Newman, and Nat Hentoff, to name a few, as well as the *New York Times*, backed RFK's Republican opponent Kenneth Keating. RFK, however, won easily.

One notable step in his campaign was his speech to that year's Democratic Party Convention. According to Schlesinger's account, "When Kennedy was finally introduced to the convention, I stood on the floor in the midst of the thunderous ovation. I had never seen anything like it. He repressed his tears. Many in the audience did not. RFK spoke for 22 minutes and ended with the quotation from *Romeo and Juliet*:

> When he shall die
> Take him and cut him out in little stars
> And he will make the face of heaven so fine
> That all the world will be in love with night,
> And pay no worship to the garish sun.

In the U.S. Senate

While in the U.S. Senate, Robert Kennedy took up the issues that were ripping America apart—poverty, especially in the Black community, and the war in Vietnam.

His deep commitment to the poor is reported in the book *Robert Kennedy. His Life*. Author Evan Thomas writes of a trip RFK took in 1967 to Mississippi, as a member of the Senate Labor Committee's newly created sub-committee on housing. He went to rural Mississippi to hold hearings. He went out into the fields; there he was deeply moved by scenes of the abject squalor in which people lived. That same night, when he flew home to New York accompanied by his aides, one of the aides writes, "he grabbed me. He said, 'You don't know what I saw! I have done nothing in my life!

Senator Robert Kennedy visits the Mississippi Delta in 1967.

Everything I have done is worthless!'"

The very evening that he returned home from his Mississippi trip, he called together his nine children, ages two to fifteen, and demanded that they must dedicate their lives to better the world. He told them what he had seen. Author Thomas writes that he told his children that on the trip he had gone into one windowless shack. He sat down on a dirty floor and held a child who was covered with open sores. He rubbed the child's stomach, which was distended by starvation. He caressed and murmured and tickled, but got no response. The child was in a daze. He told his children:

> In Mississippi, a whole family lives in a shack the size of this room. The children are covered with sores and their tummies stick out because they have no food. Do you know how lucky you are? Do you know how lucky you are? Do something for your country!

In the Senate, RFK, following in the path of FDR, sponsored a public works bill to create two million jobs. He wanted to create jobs that built something, though the general sentiment was just to hand out poverty funds to the ghetto. But with all the money needed for the war in Vietnam, Johnson sank the bill.

On March 2, 1967, RFK publicly broke with President Johnson on the question of Vietnam. In a Senate speech he called the war a horror, and called for a bombing pause to test Hanoi's sincerity on wanting peace. The press responded by launching a savage campaign against him. The next day RFK was accused by J. Edgar Hoover's leaker, columnist Drew Pearson, of being behind a failed attempt on the life of Castro, a story that Pearson had been sitting on for months.

RFK then went onto the university campuses speaking out against the war. He challenged those students with deferments who did nothing, while the poor did the fighting and dying, asking them, "Why should the poor have to do the fighting while they, as middle class students, get deferments?"

In the spring of 1967, Martin Luther King joined in opposing the war. That summer he began collaborating with RFK. Kennedy proposed to King that poor people all over the country come to Washington. This was the origin of the Poor Peoples Campaign. King said to a friend that, with Johnson out, "We have to get behind Bobby now that he's in."

'Tame the Savageness of Man'

Kennedy was on a plane heading for a campaign rally in Indianapolis, when he was told that King was shot dead on April 4, 1968. He was told to call off the rally as his security was at risk. The chief of police warned him not to go into the ghetto. Kennedy went anyway. His police escort abandoned him as he entered the ghetto. The crowd that gathered had not heard the news of MLK's death. Kennedy told them. Kennedy's speech that informed them ended:

> Let us dedicate ourselves to what the Greeks wrote so many years ago: to tame the savageness of man and to make gentle the life of this world.
> Let us dedicate ourselves to that, and say a prayer for our country and for our people.

Over the next days there were riots in 110 cities. Thirty-nine people were killed, mostly black. There were 75,000 troops in the street. But there were no riots in Indianapolis where Kennedy was campaigning. Kennedy continued to speak out, in Cleveland and elsewhere.

Schlesinger writes:

> He flew back to Washington, a city of smoke and flame, under curfew, patrolled by troops. He walked through the black districts. Burning wood and broken glass were all over the place, said Walter Fauntroy. The troops were on duty. A crowd gathered behind us, following Bobby Kennedy. The troops saw us coming at a distance, and they put on gas masks and got their guns at the ready, waiting for this horde of blacks coming up the street. When they saw it was Bobby Kennedy, they took off their gas masks and let us through. They looked awfully relieved.

The horrors of Vietnam, 1965.

U.S. government

During the worst of the ghetto riots in 1967, Kennedy, although advised not to, had toured the black and Hispanic areas. Many welcomed him as someone who truly cared for their condition, despite their knowing that he came from one of the wealthiest families in the U.S. On Hoover's advice, Johnson sent tanks and paratroopers into Detroit. When asked what he would do if he were President, Kennedy said he would make the media show what it was like to live in the ghettos. He said:

> Let them show the sound, the feel, the hopelessness, and what it's like to think you'll never get out. Show a black teenager, told by some radio jingle to stay in school, looking at his older brother—who stayed in school who is out of a job. Show the Mafia pushing narcotics; put a candid camera team in a ghetto school and watch what a rotten system of education it really is. Film a mother staying up all night to keep the rats from her baby.... Then ask people to watch it... and experience what it was like to live in the most affluent society in history—without hope.

Arthur Schlesinger quotes further trenchant remarks by RFK on the race question. Kennedy pointed to the problem of discrimination in the North which, unlike the South, had no laws against blacks. He writes:

> But the many brutalities of the North receive no attention. I have been in tenements in Harlem in the past several weeks where the smell of rats was so strong that it is difficult to stay there for five minutes, and where children slept with lights turned on their feet to discourage attacks.... Thousands do not flock to Harlem to protest these condition—much less to change them. FDR Jr. said that Kennedy was the torchbearer of everything my mother stood for and fought for.

Get Out of Vietnam

Robert Kennedy, like his brother, was being advised by General Douglas MacArthur. Both were determined to end the war in Viet Nam.

On Jan 31, 1967, RFK met with Charles DeGaulle in Paris. DeGaulle said to him:

> "I am an old man, and I have lived through many

battles and wear many scars, so listen to me closely.... Do not become embroiled in the difficulty in Vietnam."

Kennedy met with Pope Paul VI, who told him that the North Vietnamese had changed their attitude and were willing to negotiate.

President Johnson met with RFK when he returned from Europe and told him that the war would be over in a few months. RFK's response was, "These guys are out of their minds." Johnson said to him: "I'll destroy you and every one of your dove friends in six months. You'll be dead politically in six months."

Martin Luther King's funeral procession in Atlanta.

In December 1967, as Johnson was escalating bombing in North Vietnam, RFK spoke at a Catholic girls college. Kennedy was appalled when a majority wanted more, not less bombing.

Schlesinger writes:

He said to them, 'Do you understand what that means?' He cried, 'It means you are voting to send people, Americans and Vietnamese, to die.... Don't you understand what they are doing to the Vietnamese is not very different than what Hitler did to the Jews?'

Kennedy grew more vehement against the war. He said on "Face the Nation," on Nov. 26, 1967:

Do we have the right in the United States to say we're going to kill tens of thousands of people, make millions of people, as we have... refugees, kill women and children? I very seriously question whether we have that right.... Those of us who stay in the United States, we must feel it when we use napalm, when a village is destroyed and civilians are killed. This is our responsibility.

In February 1968, he gave a speech in Chicago denouncing the war. Columnist Joseph Alsop denounced him as a traitor.

This was at a time when polls showed seventy per cent of the American people backed the bombing. Kennedy said to Arthur Schlesinger:

It's just like Hitler—not a very good comparison—but I mean the way people who think themselves good and decent, become accomplices.

The Presidential Campaign

A few months before his murder in June 1968, Robert Kennedy had begun his campaign for the Presidency of the United States.

The Vietnam war issue played a major role in his decision. A commission was taking shape, with White House backing, called the Vietnam Commission. It would include members of the Supreme Court. Johnson did not appoint Kennedy. Kennedy said of this:

It was unmistakably clear to me that as long as Lyndon Johnson was President, our Vietnam policy would consist of only more war, more troops, more killing and more senseless destruction of the country we were there supposedly to save. That night I decided to run for President. (Memorandum of Clark Clifford March 14, 1968 Johnson Papers)

Soon afterwards, also in March, LBJ announced he was not running for President.

Evan Freed

Robert Kennedy campaigns for President in Los Angeles.

huge enthusiastic crowds of supporters, sometimes having parts of his clothing torn off by his fans. The press reported that Johnson hated Kennedy for his meddling, but in the middle of Kennedy's relationship with Johnson was the duplicitous FBI chief, J. Edgar Hoover. By keeping Kennedy and Johnson at each others' throats, Hoover killed two birds with one stone. Hoover unleashed a media slander campaign against RFK, accusing him of collaborating with the North Vietnamese.

RFK's friend Stewart Udall described his attitude toward the campaign as follows:

> You could tell his mind was already made up.... I almost got the feeling it was like a Greek tragedy in the sense that events themselves have been determined by fates setting the stage, and that there was really no choice left. McGovern thought Kennedy was almost oblivious to what we were saying, that he was alone in his thought.

Udall continued:

> With all the turmoil in the country and what he felt was a need for definition of the issues and for the championing of the people who were unchampioned.... He was determined to follow his own convictions and to do what was true in terms of his own personality.

On June 4, 1968 Kennedy won the California primary for President. Shortly after midnight, he was shot.

Less than a month later came the major shock of Martin Luther King's assassintion.

In Atlanta, at King's funeral there was a march, afterwards, in which Richard Nixon, Nelson Rockefeller, and Eugene McCarthy participated. One civil rights fighter there said, the only two people who were cheered by onlookers were Sammy Davis Jr and RFK. Afterwards, Ralph Abernathy, King's successor at SCLC, said:

> I was so despondent and frustrated at King's death, I had to seriously ask myself—Can this country be saved? I guess the thing that kept us going was that maybe Bobby Kennedy would come up with some answers for the country.... I remember telling him he had a chance to be a prophet. But prophets get shot." (Arthur Schlesinger, p. 879)

Kennedy had campaigned tirelessly and received tremendous popular support. Despite numerous death threats, he continuously risked his life, wading into

Short Bibliography:

1. Arthur Schlesinger. *Bobby Kennedy and His Times.* Houghton Mifflin, 1978.
2. Evan Thomas. *Robert Kennedy: His Life.* Simon and Schuster, 2000.
3. Robert Kennedy. *Robert Kennedy In His Own Words.* Bantam Press, 1988.
4. William J. Rust. *Kennedy in Viet Nam.* Scribner, New York, 1985.

December 1971: LaRouche Stopped British Takeover

by Gerald Rose

May 24—It is hard for people today to imagine the stunning impact of the total vindication of Lyndon LaRouche's forecast that day— Aug. 15, 1971—when Richard Nixon pulled the dollar out of the Bretton Woods system by severing it from the gold-reserve standard. Within hours, the headquarters of the Labor Committees—LaRouche's political organization—were flooded with phone calls recognizing LaRouche as the only economist on the planet who had forecast the end of liberal economic theory. All of the "built-in stabilizers" had failed, and in order to stabilize the dollar, Treasury Secretary John Connally had declared wage-and-price controls for the first time since World War II.

EIRNS/Alan Yue

Leading Keynesian economist Prof. Abba Lerner of NYU in debate with Lyndon LaRouche (seated, left) on Dec. 2, 1971. The shocking British "coup" of Aug. 15 that year had forced Nixon to break up the Bretton Woods System—LaRouche, alone, had forecast it.

On Sept. 30, 1971, over a thousand people gathered at Columbia University to hear a lecture by LaRouche on what had just happened.

Paul Samuelson, 1970 Nobel Prize winner, and the leading economist of the post-war period, wrote in his *Economics: An Introductory Analysis*: "The modern fiscal system has great inherent automatic stabilizing properties. All through the day and night, whether or not the President is to be found in the White House, the fiscal system is helping to keep our economy stable."

An editorial in the Aug. 30, 1971 issue of the LaRouche organization's newspaper *Solidarity* was headlined, "100% Off: Experts for Sale Cheap." Both the "conservative" economists and those of the "Left"

had agreed a breakdown crisis was impossible. Only LaRouche had forecast in the late 1960s that this breakdown—which, he had specified, would include the breakup of Bretton Woods—was not only possible, but inevitable, given the policies that were being pursued.

And, in the same forecasts, LaRouche had foreseen that the breakup of the Bretton Woods system would be accompanied by fascist measures against the living standards of the labor force.

Now this had actually occurred. The British had ended the Bretton Woods system, and with it the credit system that had dominated the post-war development of Europe and Asia. We had gone to a floating-exchange-rate system. In the wake of the British assassination of President John F. Kennedy, this was designed to destroy the United States.

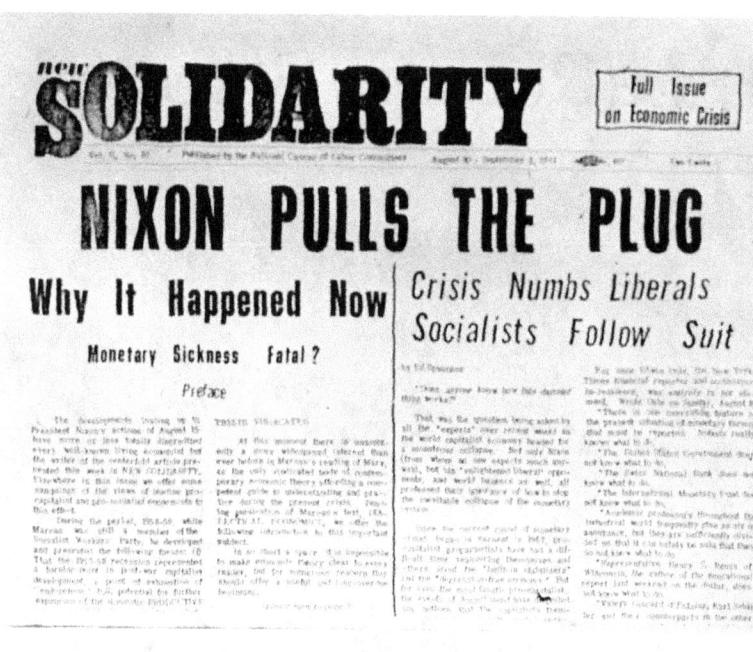

This is the context in which LaRouche's debate with Prof. Abba Lerner, took place on Dec. 2, 1971 at Queens College in New York City.

The Debate Begins

LaRouche, the individual genius who had come seemingly out of nowhere, had become one of the most prominent economists in the country. He had forecast the 1957-58 U.S. recession as well as the 1971 breakdown crisis. It was no wonder that Abba Lerner, the leading Keynesian economist and visiting professor at Queens College, would have to debate Lyndon LaRouche. It became clear later that Prof. Sydney Hook of New York University and the Hoover Institution, one of the founders of the Congress for Cultural Freedom in the United States, and others, had chosen Lerner to try and stop LaRouche.

A big mistake, as Hook was later to admit.

Lerner had taken courses with John Maynard Keynes himself at the London School of Economics and was a student of New Left economist Paul Sweezy, who was also a leading Keynesian. Lerner had supported Nixon's pulling the dollar off the gold reserve standard, and the imposition of wage-and-price controls. Lerner, a radical leftist, had supported the Brazilian junta in imposing wage-and-price controls, though he did not like the totalitarian "Bonapartist" regime that

did it. Both Left and Right had agreed that the "restraints" of the Bretton Woods system had to be gotten rid of.

These moves were a direct takeover of the U.S. economy by the British.

Only LaRouche immediately understood the fascist implications of these policies. At Queens College, he drew Lerner out on just that question.

Lerner started the debate with the simple Keynesian description of "inflation as too much money chasing too few goods." He went on to insist that by wage-and-price controls, you could increase employment, and that more people at work would create more demand, and that by freeing the dollar from the gold-reserve standard, you could print more dollars as employment rose. He made the argument that it was too high wages for productive workers, which had caused the inflation.

LaRouche's response should be quoted in full:

"The trouble … which Professor Lerner doesn't seem to grasp, is that, in the ordinary course of events, economic teaching in universities, is more like the practice of a priesthood than anything to do with reality. It's simply something you learn, you don't use it in business much; in point of fact, most business economists, or, most practicing economists in business, do not have an economics training, but usually an industrial engineering, or some other type of training. However, in the course of the crisis, these abstractions, which are the priestly affairs of economics education—which you have to learn to pass the course, primarily—become something more than abstractions. They become something related to concrete policies which affect the *lives of people*. And, they have consequences for people.

"And thus, people who are too divorced from reality, seeing these abstractions merely as innocent intellectual toys, lack a grasp of the blood-concreteness that these abstractions sometimes lead to in practice; and therefore, since the lives and well-beings of millions, and even billions of people are at stake, that an error in the domain of abstraction, is not an intellectual error; it can be a bloody crime against humanity.

"A professor who says innocently, 'The economy,

from my point of view, would be better organized if certain administrative arrangements were made,' does not necessarily think *out*, to the kind of administrative arrangements which in practice *realize* that very innocent practice. Professor Lerner may attempt to divorce his economic policies from the policies of the government of Brazil, and see them in abstraction and detachment from that; however, you can not carry out the economic policies, which are recommended for Brazil, without having the kind of government which makes those economic policies work. You could not have the kind of policies which are recommended, which he has recommended as a classic austerity policy for increased unemployment.

"Now, this is classic, in the sense that this is precisely the policy of Schacht [German central banker and Hitler's Economics Minister Hjalmar Schacht—ed.] from 1933, on, in Germany, in which wages were frozen to prevent the inflation, and in order to increase employment. He may personally detach himself from that, but it's not possible for the politicians to accept his advice, to detach themselves from the kind of government, and the kind of procedures, which enable those abstractions to become reality.

"And, that has to be grasped; because, now, no longer is economics merely a plaything of an obscure corner of the academic priesthood. Now economic policy is that which determines the lives, and daily lives and conditions of people. The form of economic policy, determines the kind of government, which is necessary to carry it out. And, the only kind of government which can carry out the kind of policy which Professor Lerner recommends—in all well-meaning, all good intention—would have to be a Bonapartist or fascist government.

"He may be opposed to fascism with every fiber of

From the Debate: LaRouche on Schacht

"If there is future real production to meet this promissory note, all is well. However, if production is declining, relative to the rate of expansion of these promissory notes, then obviously what you get into is a simple process of refinancing promissory notes. And, when this refinancing process reaches the point of inflation that threatens long-term credit, then the refinancing of these promissory notes means the conversion—or, it tends to mean conversion—of long-term credit into short-term credit.

"And that, of course, leads to bankruptcy, which is precisely the problem we face, that when you get bankrupt, you hock somebody; maybe your grandmother, if you're a certain kind of businessman. And, essentially what the capitalist system is proposing to do, is to hock the wages of the working class to pay these promissory notes, under conditions in which it is no longer possible to issue the damn things.

"That's precisely what Schacht did.

"As I said, Professor Lerner attempts to divorce, again, Schacht's proposal from the kind of government that Schacht represented. The reason the German financiers supported Hitler, was not because they had any affection for Hitler. No capitalist, no financier, no Rockefeller, wants some pig like Göring coming in and grabbing up whole sections of his industry; or support legions of SS. But, if that's the only way that the policy that Professor Lerner proposes can be implemented, and people run to it; if there is a fascist school in the United States, then the American financiers will support it, just as they did Hitler—not because the abstraction itself seems to imply a fascist state, but in order to impose these policies on the working class, the working class has to be atomized and suppressed; and there is only—under modern systems, there are only two kinds of government that do that:

"In an underdeveloped country, you can do it with a Bonapartist regime, like that in Brazil. In the advanced sector, where you have a very large working class, which is well organized, which has a trade-union tradition, you can break the working class only by atomizing it and suppressing it.

"And therefore, the *only* way that the kind of policies that Professor Lerner is talking about can be carried out, is by a Brüning and von Papen regime, succeeded by a Hitler regime, or its equivalent in the United States.

"And that's what the practical issue is."

his being; this was also true in Germany, where many economists, liberal economists, proposed austerity, who also opposed the Nazi regime. But, nonetheless, there are men who will take up these policies and carry them out, and they will be Bonapartists or fascists; but not Professor Lerner. So, he must understand, that sometimes his good intentions do not insure, that his policies, carried into practice, will work out as he sees them, in human terms."

No Fascist Economics Without a Hitler

Professor Lerner attempted again to defend his thesis: "I would agree with that. If by Capitalism I mean, the kind of behavior or policies which are responsible for the depression of the '30s. We said [then], we must not print any more money, even if it is needed, because we don't have gold.

"Now, among the people who did not do this, was Adolf Hitler, who in fact increased prosperity in Germany, gave people jobs; and if it's so, I don't think it is funny, for it was very unfortunate, for these good things led people to support him...."

LaRouche interjected, "That is precisely what Schacht did . . . and that is what the practical issue is."

There had been no *faux pas* on Lerner's part. Indeed, his mentor, John Maynard Keynes, in the preface to the 1936 German edition of his book, *General Theory of Employment, Interest, and Money*, had stated that "The theory of output as a whole, which is what the following book purports to provide, is much more easily adapted to the conditions of a totalitarian state."

Yet on a more profound level, LaRouche had demonstrated that inflation is caused by the severing of *useful economic production* from money, and the heaping of debt service and speculation on production—*not* increases in labor costs. It is to be noted that within 15 days of the Aug. 15, 1971 attack on the United States,

Finance Minister Hjalmar Schacht looked uncomfortable with his dictator. Schacht's Keynesian "MeFo Bills" policy created employment at declining wages during the mid-1930s. Could his "liberal fascism" be separated from Hitler's Nazis?

LaRouche had written a newspaper article, "Why the Monetary Crisis Happened," read by political activists around the country. It included a clear discussion of the profound difference between money and value in the economy as a whole.

It is precisely monetarism, LaRouche wrote, that caused fascism in the attempt to defend "values" that had no basis in real productivity or energy flux densities. These fictitious values had to be looted from labor, capital, and farm incomes, and finally, in Nazi Germany, from the very bodies of the labor force itself, in hard labor on 1,000 calories a day: "The Final Solution."

'Liberal' Fascism

At the end of the debate, Lerner was forced to defend his position with a fatal claim: that "If Germans had listened to Schacht, then they wouldn't have needed Hitler."

This attempt to defend Schacht's "liberal fascism" brought a gasp from debate audience.

Two weeks later, Prof. Sidney Hook was confronted on Lerner's admission. Hook indicated he knew what had happened, and swore that LaRouche would never get another debate on any campus in the country.

LaRouche went on to forecast the political demise of President Nixon, since it had been he who was used to sever the last relationship to Franklin Roosevelt, in an assault on the institution of the Presidency. Nixon was the fall-guy of George Shultz and Henry Kissinger, LaRouche wrote, both of them, admitted British agents.

I have interviewed several participants at that debate. Their universal impression was that LaRouche was not making "debaters' points," but was forcing Lerner deeper and deeper into the actual argument, and ruthlessly pursuing the truth of the issue. Those interviewed were all individuals who said they had joined LaRouche's movement after that debate—a demonstration of the power of truth.

LaRouche's SDI: A U.S.-Soviet Agreement for Peace and Development

by Jeffrey Steinberg

May 23—In early 1977, a group of patriotic U.S. intelligence officials, mostly veterans of the wartime OSS, approached Lyndon La-Rouche and embarked on a nearly 40-year collaboration that persists to this day. Although they were attached to different agencies—some official, some private—they were all part of the institution of the U.S. Presidency.

The immediate trigger of the approach was LaRouche's election-eve 1976 half-hour prime-time TV broadcast, in which he warned, as the U.S. Labor Party's Presidential candidate, that a vote for Jimmy Carter was a vote for a Trilateral Commission apparatus that was committed to a thermonuclear confrontation with the Soviet Union. The LaRouche broadcast detailed the agenda and personnel of the Trilateral Commission and warned, prophetically, that a Carter victory would usher the Trilaterals into every key national security, foreign policy, and economic post within the government.

The message these patriots delivered to LaRouche was blunt: His assessment of the takeover of the White House by the Trilateral Commission was correct, and he was asked to be part of a patriotic resistance to the genuine danger of thermonuclear war.

LaRouche was not a newcomer to the U.S. Presidency. As an Army Medical Corps soldier in the China-Burma-India theater in World War II, he had strongly reacted to the death of President Franklin Roosevelt in April 1945 with a warning that a "great President" had been lost, and had been replaced by a "little man," Harry S Truman.

Back in the United States in 1948, he had written to Gen. Dwight David Eisenhower, urging him to run for President that year as a Democratic Party candidate. Eisenhower had responded in writing to LaRouche, ex-

Lyndon LaRouche on national television, Nov. 1, 1976

youtube

plaining that he was not yet ready to run for President, but appreciated the message of encouragement. After spending the 1950s and early 1960s battling against the scourge of McCarthyism, LaRouche had plunged into political activism in the 1960s, in the wake of the assassination of President John F. Kennedy. In August 1971, he had warned, in an editorial in the weekly newspaper *New Solidarity*, which he had founded, that when Nixon pulled the plug on the Bretton Woods System, he had doomed his own Presidency, and had set the United States on a course of economic ruin through rampant Wall Street speculative looting of the real economy.

The early 1977 approach, effectively co-opting him into a position within the institution of the U.S. Presidency, was an upgrading of an already long-standing relationship with the powers and responsibilities of the Executive Branch of the U.S. Federal government. La-Rouche was more than ready to fulfill those responsibilities.

The Strategic Defense Initiative Vision

In May 1977, *Aviation Week* published an account of Gen. George Keegan's assessment that the Soviet Union had made significant breakthroughs in particle-beam lasers, which could give Moscow a strategic edge in developing defensive systems against incoming thermonuclear weapons. LaRouche, who had earlier founded the Fusion Energy Foundation, saw the merits in General Keegan's warnings. Keegan had recently retired as the head of U.S. Air Force Intelligence, and had earned a reputation as an independent, hard-nosed strategic analyst.

Through his newly established ties to key patriotic segments of the U.S. intelligence community, LaRouche directly intervened to launch what later came to be known as the Strategic Defense Initiative (SDI). LaRouche called for U.S.-Soviet collaboration to fully explore the prospects of beam defense, and argued that such a joint Soviet-American project could bring an end to the insane doctrine of Mutually Assured Destruction (MAD), under which mankind faced a constant threat of thermonuclear annihilation.

Through the former OSS circles, and other channels, LaRouche developed lines of collaboration with Ronald Reagan, the former California Governor who was already seen as a leading contender for the 1980 Republican Party Presidential nomination. Reagan had come to the same conclusions as LaRouche about the insanity of MAD, largely through his collaboration with Dr. Edward Teller of Lawrence Livermore National Laboratory in California.

When LaRouche entered the Democratic Party Presidential primaries for 1980, he based much of his campaign on the push for beam defense collaboration with the Soviet Union. He continued his relentless campaign to expose the Trilateral Commission, now focusing his attention on another Trilateralist running for President, Republican candidate George H.W. Bush.

During a Presidential candidates debate in New Hampshire, sponsored by the National Rifle Association in early 1980, LaRouche had an opportunity to speak directly with Reagan, and the two men began a personal collaboration that would have historic consequences, culminating with President Reagan's March 23, 1983 nationwide TV address, in which he announced the launching of the Strategic Defense Initiative.

When Reagan was elected President in a landslide victory over incumbent Jimmy Carter, Reagan and his circle of close advisors further drew LaRouche into the Presidency. Beginning in early 1981, first under the auspices of the CIA, and later under the auspices of the National Security Council, LaRouche established a back-channel dialogue with high-level designated officials of the Soviet government, posted at the Soviet embassy in Washington, D.C.

The subject of the dialogue was the proposal for joint work on a new doctrine of Mutually Assured Survival, replacing MAD. LaRouche's proposal, elaborated in a series of reports by the Fusion Energy Foundation and *Executive Intelligence Review*, and presented at a series of major international conferences in Washington and in European, Asian, and South American capitals, called for a revolution in science and physical economy—and an end to the Cold War on mutually beneficial terms. LaRouche, still living in New York City, made frequent trips to Washington throughout 1981-1983, meeting with his Soviet counterpart, and then reporting in person to a senior official of the National Security Council (NSC), Richard Morris, who was a top aide to National Security Advisor Judge William Clark. Written reports were submitted to the NSC on all of the trips.

In 1988, testifying as a character witness for LaRouche in Federal Court in Alexandria, Va., Richard Morris told the court that LaRouche and his associates had been involved in seven classified national security projects on behalf of the Reagan Administration—including the SDI.

On March 23, 1983, Ronald Reagan concluded a nationwide television address from the Oval Office with the following announcement:

> In recent months ... my advisors ... have underscored the necessity to break out of a future that relies solely on offensive retaliation for our security. Over the course of these discussions, I have become more and more deeply convinced that the human spirit must be capable of rising above dealing with other nations and human beings by threatening their existence. Wouldn't it be better to save lives than to avenge them? Are we not capable of demonstrating our peaceful intentions by applying all our abilities and our ingenuity to achieving a truly lasting stability? I think we are—indeed we must!
>
> After careful consultation with my advisors, including the Joint Chiefs of Staff, I believe

Ronald Reagan Presidential Library

President Reagan announces the SDI on national television, March 23, 1983.

their great talents now to the cause of mankind and world peace; to give us the means of rendering these nuclear weapons impotent and obsolete.... We seek neither military superiority nor political advantage. Our only purpose—one all people share—is to search for ways to reduce the danger of nuclear war.

President Reagan concluded his historic message with a note of cautious optimism:

My fellow Americans, tonight we are launching an effort that holds the promise of changing the course of human history. There will be risks, and results take time, but I believe we can do it. As we cross this threshold, I ask for your prayers and your support.

Lyndon LaRouche immediately congratulated President Reagan for his courageous announcement, declaring:

For the first time since the end of the 1962 Cuban Missile Crisis, there is, at last, hope that the thermonuclear nightmare will be ended during the remainder of this decade. Only high-level officials of government, or a private citizen as intimately knowledgeable of details of the international political and strategic situation as I am privileged to be, can even begin to foresee the earth-shaking impact the President's television address last night will have throughout the world.

Under instructions from President Reagan, days after the March 23, 1983 speech, Defense Secretary Caspar Weinberger formally conveyed a proposal to the Soviet

there is a way. Let me share with you a vision of the future which offers hope. It is that we embark on a program to counter the awesome Soviet missile threat with measures that are defensive. Let us turn to the very strength in technology that spawned our great industrial base.... What if free people could live secure in the knowledge that their security did not rest upon the threat of instant U.S. retaliation to deter a Soviet attack; that we could intercept and destroy strategic ballistic missiles before they reach our own soil or that of our allies?... Isn't it worth every investment necessary to free the world from the threat of nuclear war? We know it is!

...I clearly recognize that defensive systems have limitations and raise certain problems and ambiguities. If paired with offensive systems, they can be viewed as fostering an aggressive policy and no one wants that. But with these considerations firmly in mind, I call upon the scientific community in our country, those who gave us nuclear weapons, to turn

1983 pamphlet by LaRouche's National Democratic Policy Committee

government, that the two nations work together to develop and deploy a strategic ballistic missile defense system.

Backlash

Even before President Reagan's historic speech, forces in London, Moscow, and Washington were moving, with increasing desperation, to preempt the President from launching his Strategic Defense Initiative.

In Moscow, the attitude towards the LaRouche back-channel shifted markedly, when General Secretary Leonid Brezhnev died in November 1982, and was replaced by the long time KGB Director Yuri Andropov. Although Andropov took ill in mid-1983 and died on Feb. 9, 1984, his brief tenure as Soviet leader coincided with the Reagan SDI offer.

Ronald Reagan Presidential Library

Attempted assassination of President Reagan, March 30, 1981

For a variety of reasons elaborated by LaRouche's Soviet interlocutor, Mr. Shershnev, Andropov rejected the Reagan offer. In part, Andropov feared that the United States would go through a surge of scientific and technological breakthroughs that would be absorbed into the overall civilian economy in ways that would leave the Soviet Union in the dust. He had also received air-tight guarantees from leading British and American policy-makers, including Henry Kissinger, Walter Mondale, and the Bush family, that Reagan would be blocked from adopting the SDI program, so closely associated with Lyndon LaRouche.

Even after the Reagan SDI speech, the Soviets continued to receive assurances that the program would be blocked from within the U.S. government. Instead of embracing the Reagan offer of SDI collaboration, Moscow adopted a hostile-aggressive policy of opposition, which included a barrage of media slanders against Lyndon LaRouche, including demands for his elimination.

Years later, Richard Morris confirmed to this author that, on the day of the SDI speech by the President, James Baker III, then President Reagan's Chief of Staff, had attempted to sabotage the delivery of the missile defense remarks, removing them from the final draft of the President's speech just hours before the scheduled television address. National Security Advisor Clark, in a total breach of protocol, bypassed Baker and went directly to the President to encourage him to restore the three-minute segment in the speech. Reagan readily agreed with Clark.

But the last ditch effort by Baker, reflecting Bush's adamant opposition to SDI, had its consequences. From the very outset, the LaRouche-Reagan-Teller plan for a joint American-Soviet scientific collaboration on new-physical-principle systems of missile defense was sabotaged—from the inside and from the outside—at every turn.

Bush versus LaRouche

There are still unanswered questions surrounding the choice of George H.W. Bush as Ronald Reagan's Vice Presidential running mate in the 1980 elections. Like LaRouche, Reagan had been a harsh public critic of the Trilateral Commission and its policies of controlled disintegration of the world economy. Bush had been an active member of the Trilateral Commission, right up to the eve of his own 1980 campaign for the GOP nomination. Yet, at the Republican nominating convention, after rejecting a proposal to name Gerald Ford as his running mate in what was publicly characterized as a Co-Presidency arrangement, Reagan was persuaded to name Bush as a lesser evil. It was a tragic, and unnecessary error, as Reagan was vastly popular and virtually assured of a landslide victory—without a Ford or Bush on the ticket.

On March 30, 1981, Ronald Reagan was shot by John Hinckley as he exited the Washington Hilton Hotel. President Reagan had only been in office 69 days when he was nearly killed by an assassin. Although the

George H.W. Bush accepts the Republican nomination as President, August 18, 1988.

President survived the shooting, it left him weakened, and this provided the opening for the Bush team to assert more and more control over the Reagan Presidency, as time passed. The ability of the Bush faction to sabotage the Reagan-LaRouche SDI collaboration was but the most consequential element of an internal sabotage of the Reagan Presidency.

The anger of the Bush apparatus, including the neo-conservatives, at LaRouche and his successful partnership with President Reagan, led to the launching of a bogus criminal investigation into LaRouche and his associates, culminating in the Oct. 6-7, 1986 raids on LaRouche offices in Leesburg, Virginia by over 400 Federal, state, and local law enforcement officers, backed up by U.S. military SWAT units. A personal communication from LaRouche to President Reagan, as well as an intervention by La-Rouche's allies within the U.S. intelligence services and the Presidency, prevented a bloodbath and the assassination of La-Rouche.

The raid, however, represented the end of the Reagan Presidency for all practical purposes. Reagan's last act on behalf of the shared strategic agenda with La-Rouche took place in the very week that the Leesburg raids were taking place. In Reykjavik, Iceland for a summit with then-Russian General Secretary Mikhail Gorbachov, an Andropov protégé, Reagan rejected Gorbachov's plea to abandon the SDI, in return for an agreement to sharply reduce the nuclear weapons arsenals. True to his commitments to the LaRouche beam defense proposal, Reagan refused to abandon his vision of Mutually Assured Survival and the new physical principles revolution at the heart of the proposal.

The battle over the Strategic Defense Initiative was a battle inside the institution of the Presidency. Lyndon LaRouche forged a policy alliance with the President on an historic mission that altered the course of history. While the SDI was sabotaged from being fully realized, by the treachery of Yuri Andropov, Henry Kissinger, George H.W. Bush, and others, the legacy of that effort would play out later, during the Bill Clinton Presidency, when LaRouche was once again called upon to serve as a critical channel to Russian scientific and governmental circles who understood the great, lost opportunity of 1983, and sought to revive the spirit of collaboration between Washington and Moscow under different circumstances, but on the basis of the same principles.

October 1986 assault on LaRouche headquarters in Leesburg, Va.

LaRouche: Declassified DIA Documents Can Bring Down Obama Now!

by Jeffrey Steinberg

May 26—Newly released "Secret" Defense Intelligence Agency documents from 2012 prove that President Obama knew that the Sept. 11, 2012 attack on the U.S. Mission and CIA Annex in Benghazi, Libya, which resulted in the murders of Ambassador Christopher Stevens and three other American officials, was a premeditated attack by a local al-Qaeda/Muslim Brotherhood affiliate. The DIA document, dated Sept. 12, 2012—just hours after the deadly attack—circulated widely among American national security officials, including to the White House, and showed, conclusively, that the assault on the U.S. diplomatic compound and CIA annex was known to have been an al-Qaeda operation.

As the result of the May 18 release of that DIA document, along with more than 100 pages of Defense and State Department "Secret" documents, the evidence is now conclusive: President Barack Obama willfully lied to the American people and to the U.S. Congress, to cover up the fact that the United States had been attacked by an al-Qaeda organization that the President had claimed was defeated, as a key feature of his Presidential re-election campaign.

The President has been caught committing "high crimes and misdemeanors" against the U.S. Constitution. He must be impeached immediately.

After being informed of the release of the DIA documents, as the result of a Freedom of Information Act (FOIA) lawsuit by Judicial Watch, Lyndon LaRouche declared that "the preconditions for President Obama's removal from office have now been met. The evidence is conclusive, and is now in the public domain."

LaRouche stated that the release of the DIA "smoking gun" will drive President Obama to "acts of desperation. His regime is about to be dumped."

The DIA "Secret" document stated, in part:

The attack on the American consulate in Benghazi was planned and executed by the Brigade of Captive Omar Abdul Rahman (BCOAR). BCOAR is also responsible for past attacks on the Red Cross in Benghazi and the attack on the British ambassador. They have approximately 120 members. The BCOAR are connected to Ansar al Sharia katiba, commanded by Sufian al GUMMA.

…The attack was planned ten or more days prior on approximately 01 September 2012. The intention was to attack the consulate and to kill

The premeditated burning of the U.S. Mission in Benghazi, Libya on Sept. 11, 2012

rt/youtube

as many Americans as possible, to seek revenge for the U.S. killing of Aboyahiye ALALIBY in Pakistan and in memorial of the 11 September 2001 attack on the World Trade Center buildings.

The leader of BCOAR is Abdul Baset AZUZ, AZUZ was sent by ZAWARI to set up al-Qaeda (AQ) bases in Libya.

Other DIA documents, released as part of the FOIA action. included an October 2012 report, documenting the flow of weapons from Benghazi into the hands of jihadist Syrian rebels. Another DIA report from August 2012 documented the strong al-Qaeda and Muslim Brotherhood ties of the leading Syrian opposition groups, and actually anticipated the creation of an Islamic State on the border region of Syria and Iraq.

The question now before the U.S. Congress and the American people, is whether the mandate for Obama's impeachment will be acted on, before a major catastrophe, including, potentially, thermonuclear war, is unleashed by a desperate Obama.

A Unique Opportunity

LaRouche, who worked closely with Presidents Ronald Reagan and Bill Clinton on specific national security policies, noted that the release of the DIA evidence against President Obama affords a unique opportunity to revive the U.S. Presidency, which has been in a state of degeneracy since the British Crown launched its 1997-98 campaign to bring down the Clinton Presidency—at the precise moment that Clinton was initiating a major overhaul of the bankrupt global financial system. "The first consequence of the destruction of Bill Clinton was the repeal of Glass-Steagall, which was followed by eight disastrous years of the George W. Bush/Dick Cheney Administration, and now followed by the even more disastrous Obama Presidency," LaRouche said.

The new revelations offer a moment of opportunity to not only remove Obama from office by Constitutional means; but to restore the Presidency, reinstate Glass-Steagall, and begin a desperately-needed economic revival. This, LaRouche concluded, "is an opportunity that we cannot miss, if humanity is to survive."

The fact that the DIA made no effort to suppress the release of the Sept. 1, 2012 report is noteworthy. The DIA had been a prime source of critical intelligence

for Gen. Martin Dempsey, Chairman of the Joint Chiefs of Staff, that enabled the Chiefs to push back, particularly in August and September 2013, against Obama's plans to launch a massive bombing campaign against the Assad government and the Syrian Army. Based on high-quality DIA intelligence and assessments, General Dempsey argued, convincingly, that an all-out U.S. bombing campaign against the Assad forces would lead to the creation of a jihadist state on the eastern shore of the Mediterranean Sea. President Obama rescinded the attack order and turned to Congress, which was inundated with constituent calls, e-mails, and letters opposing the direct U.S. military intervention.

In the falling-out with the Obama White House and CIA Director John Brennan, according to one account by former DIA head of humint (human intelligence) Col. W. Patrick Lang, the head of the DIA, Gen. Michael Flynn, was forced out, along with his deputy.

The DIA revelations, which have now opened impeachment prospects, came amidst a long-overdue Democratic Party revolt against President Obama, over a range of issues, including his push for the Trans-Pacific Partnership (TPP) free-trade treaty.

The DIA document release also came just a week after renowned investigative journalist Seymour Hersh published a 10,000-word exposé in the *London Review of Books*, revealing that President Obama had also lied about the actual circumstances under which Osama bin Laden was located and killed.

Hersh's detailed account of how President Obama double-crossed Pakistani military leaders, who facilitated the bin Laden raid, and issued a string of "official" lies about the sources of the intelligence on bin Laden's whereabouts, the details of the firefight with al-Qaeda bodyguards that never happened, and the Saudi funding of the bin Laden "house arrest" in Abbottabad, Pakistan—all came from U.S. and Pakistani officials, with intimate knowledge of the actual raid.

Thus, both the Hersh exposé and the release of the DIA documents must be seen as the latest indication that patriotic networks inside the U.S. government have come to the same conclusion as LaRouche: It's time for Obama to be dumped.

EIR Had the Story

The just-released DIA report has made "official" what was known by *EIR* and others at the time: President Obama lied to the American people and to Con-

Obama confers with his fellow-liar on Benghazi, Susan Rice.

White House/Pete Souza

gress about a "spontaneous" attack and a "protest" against an Internet video slandering the Prophet Mohammed, knowing full well that the assault was a pre-planned action by al-Qaeda fronts headquartered in the Derna area near Benghazi. Derna was a well-known hotbed of al-Qaeda recruitment for suicide bombings and other terrorist acts.

On the morning of Sept. 12, 2012, *EIR* received an "unofficial" briefing from a longstanding U.S. government contact, detailing the armed assault on the U.S. Mission and Annex, naming Ansar al-Sharia as the main group involved in the planned and heavily armed action. Contemporaneous records exist of that conversation, and they conform to much of the detail in the recently declassified DIA report.

On Sept. 28, 2012, a senior Pentagon source confirmed to *EIR* that "the Obama White House received a detailed warning of a pending attack in advance of the Sept. 11, 2012 assault on the Benghazi consulate." According to the source, "Both the Defense Intelligence Agency and the National Security Agency provided detailed warnings to both the President and the CIA that there were attacks being planned against American targets in Benghazi."

Author Edward Klein, in his book *Blood Feud*, recounted that Secretary of State Hillary Clinton received a real-time account of the Benghazi attacks from U.S. diplomat Gregory Hicks, who was Ambassador Ste-

vens' top deputy at the Tripoli Embassy. Hicks provided the same narrative of a pre-meditated attack, with no mention of protest demonstrations or the slanderous video. Yet, according to the Klein account, President Obama personally called Clinton at 10 p.m. on Sept. 11, 2012 and ordered her to issue a press release citing the protests and the video, and making no mention of the al-Qaeda links or the pre-planned nature of the precision attacks.

Time To Invoke 25th Amendment?

It is now well known, that in the final days of the Richard Nixon Presidency, in 1974, there was sufficient concern that Nixon would order some kind of wild military provocation, that senior White House officials ordered the Joint Chiefs of Staff (JCS) to alert them before taking any action on Presidential orders. What has been generally left out of this otherwise confirmed account, is the fact that the White House officials were acting in accord with the U.S. Constitution's 25th Amendment (ratified February 1967), that provided the means to remove a President from office, if he or she were deemed physically or mentally unfit to continue to serve.

The White House officials were legitimately concerned about Nixon's mental state, and were acting in conformity with the 25th Amendment when they alerted the JCS.

There are clear parallels between those final days of the Nixon Presidency and the current situation. Lyndon LaRouche has pointedly warned that Presiderent Obama is going down, and, in desperation—and under orders from the British Monarchy—could try to launch a war against Russia, China, or both, that could lead to thermonuclear annihilation.

Anyone contemplating such an action is clinically insane, and mass-murderously so. The question is: Are there people in and around the White House who are sane enough and courageous enough to defend the country against an insane President, as was fortunately the case in the final days of Nixon?

LaRouche Fireside Chat Discussion With 500 Activists, May 21

Below are LaRouche's brief opening statement, and the complete 21 questions put to him, and his replies, during the 1.75-hour call. The call had more than 500 participants. Names have been removed.

LaRouche: Tony Papert, whom I presume you all know and revere, has presented a document (See "Mission Statement" this issue) which identifies, officially, according to our program, and I think that that will probably serve well to locate exactly where I am, and also where our organization is at this time. There are some things which are breaking developments, like the attempt at mass murder of the citizens of California, which is coming from the governor of that state, who's out there to kill practically everybody in California—which is not a nice idea, but that's what's in process now.

Lyndon LaRouche on the set of the New Paradigm show, May 2014.

LPAC-TV

So, that's where we are, and I'm in the middle of this stuff internationally. Helga's also, as you know, in this. We're a pair, as most people know; and we work together, and we work together with a lot of people in both the New York City area, and other areas adjacent to that, and down here in the dredges of this present location where I am today.

So, let's just go ahead with the thing.

The Presidential Campaign

First Question: This is J— from Michigan. I was wondering if you could give us any indication on Martin O'Malley's move toward throwing his hat in the ring for the Presidency, and if you and this organization have any direct contact with his movement.

LaRouche: You will notice that what we've gone through on the O'Malley case, and I've qualified this

and it's also in print in circulation—in an inprint document, which Tony Papert collected and presented this evening, earlier—that part is absolutely clear. We have a policy. We have a global policy, features of which include that, such as: California, the people of California and beyond, are now in the process of being subjected to the mass murder methods of destroying the citizenry of California. And so therefore, if the policy of the present governor of California is allowed to continue, you'll have an increasing incidence of death, and torture, among the citizens of California.

So, we're at a point where we're in a fighting situation in California. But if you look at the "Mission Statement" now, you will find that this is actually a policy which is more or less nationwide. Therefore, we have a major fight, and a fight against a crook, who is called the governor of California, who has called for mass murder, in fact, of the citizens of California.

We don't like that, and we are going to do what we can to prevent such consequences from happening to people in California, or in the the United States in general.

Second Question: This is A— from California, and I've got several questions rolling through my head. One is about Democratic politics, namely, how does it look for Bill Clinton at this point? Is he going to be helping the progressive portion of the Democratic Party get someone like O'Malley, or is he backing Hillary Clinton at this point?

LaRouche: The problem is that Mrs. Clinton is probably a lost cause. She's made too many mistakes. She's made too many submissions to Obama. And she's not really qualified to come through the process of being nominated, or elected, as President of the United States. That's the situation now.

The reality on O'Malley's case: O'Malley was always, in his political career, and in intervening periods—what he's had, he's functioned as governor earlier. He functioned on the basis of going along with going along. And he adapted himself to winning elections.

Then the time came when he shifted his orientation. Now, that doesn't mean that his personal views about life in general, have been radically changed in a progressive way. What it means is that he has gone up to the times, when what he pursued as a candidate for election, in earlier periods, he finds no longer adequate. Because what's happened is, the situation now is, the President is an enemy of the United States—that's a fact. And the Republicans are generally, with some nice exceptions, pretty much bums.

And Obama is a menace. He's an evil figure, a very evil figure. And therefore, the problem with Hillary is, she's adapted too much, to become a subject of Obama. And that's what ruined her, when she went over and accepted a position under Obama—and Obama ate her up. She is no longer the same person she was when she left to join him.

Now, I had talks with her at the time that she had entered that position—the position she gave up. But since now, she is not anywhere near competent for running for the office of President. And obviously, in general, you don't have other people who you would recommend to become President, either because you don't know they have the qualifications, or because you know they don't have the qualifications—such as the Bushes, traditionally.

So, that's where we are, in truth. We're at a point where the O'Malley option is the only one which is significantly on the table right now, for realization in the interests of the citizens of the United States.

Third Question: This is D— from Wisconsin. I want to congratulate you. You were the first one to call Scott Walker up here in Wisconsin a fascist, when nobody had the guts to do so, and they still don't have them to do so. You kind of answered my question already about Hillary, but what about Bernie Sanders? What are his shortcomings that he doesn't qualify?

LaRouche: He's not really there. He doesn't represent an active presentation which at this time is necessary. At this point, anybody who is running to be a President should, in the normal course of events, have presented a program which meets the challenge of the reality that we in the United States, and in the world in general, face. And therefore, I don't think he's a viable candidate, at least not so far, and I've seen no signs that he is a viable candidate so far. Maybe he will change. But pending a change, I think he's not a very good candidate.

Fourth Question: This is G— from Washington state. We met in 2008. I've given some information to be given to you. It's about George Bush '41. And I'd like to make certain that you're receiving it. Because you and I think a lot alike about this character and the British monarchy. But anyway, he's the first illegal alien that sat in the White House, and I can prove that. I'd like to thank you for being a patriot.

LaRouche: I think we're in a good situation. You know, I've always had, especially normally and clearly, since the beginning of the 1970s, since that time, I've been a leading, prominent public figure, and candidate for the Presidency. That has never really changed. And I think that now, despite the fact that I'm a little more aged, and not frisky and running around the way I would if I were younger; but the fact is that I probably am one of the best political authorities operating in the United States today. But I have to operate from a more modest personal position, in terms of things, because I just have to do what I have to do, as a contribution to making sure that the policy of the United States does match the requirements of the United States under these conditions.

The British Empire Is the Problem

Fifth Question: This is L— from Washington state. What do we do about the Islamic Caliphate, or at least what they claim as a Caliphate over there in the Middle East?

LaRouche: I think I can answer that directly and explicitly.

First of all, the Islamic movement based in that area, center, is only a tool of the British monarchy. It's a mass murderously inclined instrument of mass murder. That's what the Saudi operation is.

The Saudi operation is also the leading factor in genocide, throughout that entire region, that is, around the area of the Mediterranean Sea. And therefore, this is a thing which is controlled top down, and in great detail, by the British monarchy, the British Empire. So, it's merely a tool of the British terror system. And the sooner we get rid of that, the sooner people will get a chance to live.

We cannot tolerate the continuation of a British system which uses that system itself, as the means for running policy in the Mediterranean region.

Sixth Question: This is W— in Denver. I'm aware of a rumor that the U.S. is about to install some anti-missile defense system in Ukraine.

LaRouche: That's an attempt, and that is the intention of Obama. Obama is a British agent. He's got a very bad history, actually. He's a very evil person. He should never have been the President of the United States, and he should not continue to be the President of the United States at this point.

The danger to the United States and its people, and civilization generally, that Obama represents right now, is the greatest threat to the existence of human beings on this planet today.

Seventh Question: This is E— from the Bronx, New York City. I want to ask you about ISIS, or ISIL. How can we militarily defeat them now, because they're a real threat to the whole world, with their terrorist organization? How can the U.S. overthrow and militarily get rid of them right now?

U.S. State Department

Recently crowned Saudi King Salman bin Abdelaziz al Saud, holding court in May 2015, with Secretary of State John Kerry.

LaRouche: The problem is that you've got a bunch of people in the Congress, and so forth, who really are not coming up to the standard of performance which the United States desperately needs at this time. Many members of the Congress are incompetent. There are members of the Congress who also are valid, very valid people, very serious people. But we have a lot of people who are not.

The only problem in general is that the tendency among the candidates often, is that they're opportunists, and they act on the basis of what they can get for themselves, in their prospective incomes, their promotions, what they can sell out to do, what they try to sell themselves out to do, that kind of stuff. And we have a very poor quality of moral performance among the members of the Congress; not because they are inherently bad, but because they tend to capitulate to what they feel the pressures are, which determine their opportunities for promotion.

Eighth Question: This is J— from Alaska. I have a question about priorities. I sensed that our number one priority now is, we've got to get a restoration of the Presidency of the United States, get Mr. Obama out. And it seems like there's a lot of things all stacking up that should make that easy, but I'm always amazed and surprised that he's still in there. I didn't think he'd last that long. The lies about Benghazi now, and the highlighting of the 28 pages, numerous impeachable offenses—the whole warfare. The terrible foreign policy—we've got to get him out of there.

But I see a very important flank here with this water crisis going on in California, and I sense—I'm in Alaska here, and I've been kind of hoping and organizing towards the development of NAWAPA. We'd love to develop the Arctic region and there's so much potential, looking forward to the first development of Alaska. But NAWAPA seems to be on the back burner, and I understand the crisis is now, and ionization, nuclear desalination, all of these things would be the very first steps. Anyway, I wondered if you could comment about the whole priorities.

LaRouche: The answer is really a little bit of a shift in the subject the way you presented it. First of all, you cannot take a deductive approach to solutions to the problems which face us now: That most of the important issues are not on the table, and they are deliberately kept off the table.

Take the case of the area which you're probably more close to—California, Northern California, in particular, because that part of California is actually the most viable right now in this time. But, what's the policy?

You have a corruption of the governorship in California, in which the heir of a qualified leader in California, is a piece of nuisance, and worse. Now what they're doing—and this has two aspects to it. One is what these guys are doing, the ones in power, the governor and so forth. He's a useless, and worse than useless creature. He's nothing like his father. He's a bum. He's an opportunist. He's a prostitute in the sense of political prostitute. And he comes from a certain circle of prostitution in California, which came after the period of the father of the current governor. Because the earlier figure was a commendable person, in general, and did useful things.

The son has been a tragedy, for both California, and for the United States in general, because of his role and influence—what's going on now.

The problem is this. The argument on water—and I'm sure you're aware of the whole water problem as it's being presented now. The intention is, the practical intention is, to reduce the population of the United States, as well as other nations—in other words, it's a plan of mass murder of people in various parts of the world. And it's not just some people being murdered;

it's a great majority of the population of the trans-Atlantic region, and beyond—the intention, the policy in Europe, the government, the British Empire most specifically. The British Empire is a genocide case organization—it's a pro-genocide case, and always has been, under this reign.

So the issues you are confronted with are not the real issues. They are shadows of a really ugly set of issues.

"You just can't live the way you always have. For over 10,000 years, people lived in California, but the number of those people were never more than 300,000 or 400,000."

— Gov. Jerry Brown
quoted in *New York Times*, April 5, 2015

Now, right now, the issue of the water question, and the water question in the United States, and across the trans-Atlantic region, is the functional issue *right now*. It's the issue of survival of human beings. The citizens of the United States and elsewhere.

The British Empire has long had a policy of genocide, and the current incumbency of the Queen and her consort, are advocates of a kind of genocide worse than that of Adolf Hitler. And they should be looked at as the successors, or continuation, of the principles of Adolf Hitler. Hitler was just unfortunate in being defeated, but the British are still there, and they were the same thing that Hitler represented, in terms of their policy. They're no different.

Saudi Arabia is the key instrument and tool of the British Empire, and that's the case. Europe is terrified, in general, terrified by a fear of the influence of the British Empire. That's a fact.

Look, the good side, which is there, is that we have a new potentiality in Eurasia. This means China is a leader of the world. China is the most powerful, biggest nation in the world, in terms of citizenship, and it's growing fast. India has come up rapidly, as the new administration is put in place. Similar kinds of views exist in various parts of the world. South America—there are certain nations in South America which are coming up again.

So, we're looking at a point where we can throw out, expel the evil, led by the British Empire, then and now. The British Empire under this monarchy, in particular, is the most evil thing that mankind has experienced in a very long time. That has to be defeated. It has

EIRNS/Robert Baker

LaRouchePAC rallies on Wall Street, April 9, 2015.

to be defeated by nations. There are many other things about this, but the key thing that you have to recognize is this:

There is a change in the water supply, in the trans-Pacific region, and across in Europe. The water supplies needed by the population of North America, in particular, and streaming around that, is a crucial matter right now. The threat to human life in the United States on the water issue, is one of the leading issues. This is matched by the fact that the California governor and others, are actually advocates of genocide, just as much as Adolf Hitler was. A little different in approach, but the effect is pretty much the same.

So, the governor of California is a menace, and a lot of people in the Congress are also menaces on that same account. Their intention is to reduce the population of the United States greatly, at an accelerating rate, to kill off citizens of the United States in particular. Why? Over the water issue and the food issue, which are closely related.

So therefore, what we need to do is get rid of those skunks who are threatening the lives of most of you; most of the citizens of the United States are now under a very serious threat of death, coming from these sources. The water supply is being cut off. Now, the water supply being cut off in California and other locations, means early mass death within the population of California. And the present governor of California is a leader in implementing that policy.

So, the question is: are we going to fight against these forces, the so-called green forces, the green

policy? And the green policy, which has been popularized in many places, is the keystone for mass murder of the population of the United States, and of other parts of the world, around the globe. And that's what we have to deal with.

The Manhattan Project

Ninth Question: Hello Lyn, this is A—, another Bronx chorus voice calling in on this Manhattan project. And I'm a part of the so-called Manhattan Project. And we've been trying to organize ourselves now around something new and exciting that we've missed in the past, I think. And that is, reaching out to the working class of the New York City area. And I wanted to ask for your guidance on this new potential for us. It seems that—yes, and I'm a product of it—that they're, in a lot of ways, in bad shape. Yet, there are some really good people, and they need to be truly organized. And these are the folks, I think, who can help us win the day on a local and national level and spread; but it is, of course, a real challenge, and requires a lot of patience. And I was wondering if you could help us here in New York as to how we can begin to rally these individuals to our cause.

LaRouche: Well, New York essentially gives the most opportune opening for success. As a matter of fact, since August-October of last year, I have shifted the policy of our organization nationally. I don't know if all people caught up with it, but that's what I've been doing. In order to build around New York City, that is, Alexander Hamilton's legacy, as opposed to those, from the Southern parts of the United States, who were Presidents who weren't worth much. And we have a lot of Presidents on the record who ain't worth much, and never were. Only a few of them. So, that's the general problem that we face, and that's the problem we have to look at and deal with.

So, what we're doing right now, and what I've been doing since my policy turn and, you know, is saying, "Here's the solution. Go back to Alexander Hamilton." The principle of economic development and policy of the United States is that which was formulated by Alexander Hamilton. The Alexander Hamilton policy which is the policy intrinsic to all competent people in the

New York area. That's it. That's the center of the United States, New York City. And you have a spill-back from New England, for example, and some other locations.

But the basic thing here is a law, the conception of law, which was continued by Alexander Hamilton. And it is the Hamiltonian principle which we are applying to Manhattan. We're not fully on it, but we've picked out those kinds of people who represent the natural heirs of the policy typified by Alexander Hamilton—and the economic policy, and the social policy—because there were very few Presidents in the United States during that time, and even up into the present time, very few Presidents who really deserved to be Presidents. And the problem is, most of them have been weak, or just unable, or rather stupid.

And so therefore, the way we can organize and rebuild this nation is by understanding what forces in the course of the history of this nation, represent the policy-making, the policy-shaping of the United States Constitution. And the most reliable point for that single point, is probably a certain section of the Manhattan population and people around it. They are the actual implicit center of the organization needed around New York City despite all the other problems that exist. In New York City, there is a very powerful, large minority of citizens in the vicinity of Manhattan who represent the potential leadership en masse, of the recovery and rebuilding of the United States. And that's what I'm committed to. This means that we have to understand not only what that segment of the population means, we have to understand what the means are that we have to apply to make that thing work.

In other words, this is the point. When you look at the history of the United States and the Presidency, most of the Presidencies of the United States were tragedies, or worse. There've been a few great Presidents, exceptional Presidents, but in the majority, the Presidency is usually occupied by a skunk.

We Must Return to America's Legacy

Tenth Question: I'd like to know, why we have an 1848 railroad system in the United States of America, with the same gauge track that they had when they first

BRICS leaders at Fortaleza, Brazil on July 15, 2014.

BRICS official photo

put the train across the United States. Countries, even like the Soviet Union, have wide-track railway that can carry much more cargo, many more passengers. Why don't we combine the interstate highway system right of way with a railroad system to connect, and possibly make our country much more economically sound? And also reduce auto traffic and the cost of moving food and passengers. I'm calling from New York, I'm calling from the Bronx....

LaRouche: Okay. I'm aware of these things, very acutely aware of these things, and painfully, acutely aware of these things. You have to look at the history of the United States. And there's a very specific characteristic which we should call to our attention. That is, that what has happened is that, except for a handful of Presidents of the United States, a handful, a relative handful, most of the Presidents were skunks. Why? Because the British Empire, directly and indirectly, as in the case of the Confederacy, which was a British instrument. Many of these states, from Virginia on down, have never had a record of patriotism toward the United States. They are still, in the main, Southerners, and they are corrupt in that way. Not that they intend to be corrupt, but they don't know any better.

And the problem has been, we've had only a few Presidents in the history of the United States Presidency who are fit to occupy the position of President. You just look at the record. Less than about a dozen, slightly more than a dozen Presidents were actually qualified to be Presidents. Most of them weren't. They were either incompetent, or they were maliciously incompetent. So, therefore we've come to a point where we have to recognize that the United States is not just the United States in name. The point is, we're at a point where a new development is occurring around the world. It's called the BRICS. It includes Russia, it includes China, it includes India, it includes the leading nations of South America, and so forth. These are the nations which have moral viability. They may not be perfect, but they have, on balance, a moral option.

Europe is a disaster. Not because Europe has to be a disaster, but because it is made to be a disaster, and we would like to correct that. So, these are the realities. So, we've come to a point where we need to provide a leadership, and it's not a matter of how many people are involved. There has to be a leadership inside the United States and beyond, which presents to the future of mankind, the options, available options, which can remedy the disaster which has been centered, globally, around the British Empire since as long as the United States has existed. Therefore, the destruction of the British Empire and what it represents—including the Saudis. The Saudis are nothing but mass murderers, who operate under the orders of the Queen. And most of the European nations have a streak of cowardice in them which is really awesome.

So, what is needed is what we can do in terms of what the legacy of the United States. And the legacy of the United States is a real one. It can be reactivated and brought forth as a force if we want to do it. And that role of the United States and the people of the United States who represent that role, have the means available to them.

Now let's be concrete; let's take the case of O'Malley. Right now, O'Malley was, in a sense, for some time, an ordinary Presidential candidate, unqualified to be a President. But, in the recent period, he changed his role, not his intentions, but his role, because when he was running for President before, he was operating on the basis of politically practical approach to politics. Hmmm. Now when the crisis has come in, the Obama case has come in, O'Malley has gone beyond that, and with some other leading figures in our system, has recognized that there has to be a change. And if you look at what O'Malley, what he has done recently, you see those changes, visibly. Therefore, we can say that O'Malley, right now, is the clearest case of a potentially qualified President right now. All of the others are either doubtful or known to be incompetent for this purpose. And that's the way we have to think.

Now what I have to do—because I have a special role, you know. I've been an international trouble-maker against the British Empire for most of my life, and proud of it. But what we have to do, is we have to make our people, in the United States and elsewhere, sensitive, and sensible of, what we can do by our legacy. What we have to do is understand what O'Malley represents at this point. O'Malley is the only prospective Presidential candidate, on the scene now, presently. You know, there can be changes, but right now he's the only person who's really qualified to become the President of the United States. And that's because of a combination of his virtues, and his expediencies, and all these kinds of things. But he's the only fit person, fit to be a presidential candidate right now. None of the others are qualified, either because of their weaknesses, or because of what the policies are that they adopt.

Eleventh Question: Hello, this is D— from Arizona, and I wanted to bring up—I've been listening to some YouTube videos, and it brought to mind what FDR said, that Presidents are not elected, they're selected. There's a cabal up there that controls the military-industrial complex, the press, the financial oligarchy, and with that, they seem to say that, here we're giving the Republicans and Democrats, they're all part of our deal—we have an A-team on one, and a B-team on the other, and the A-team may be a Republican one election cycle, and change for the next one.

How can we overcome that, because it seems like most of the people don't care? So we have this group that selects and they give you two choices, neither of which is worth anything.

LaRouche: My view on that is, that I continue to do what I do. Because I don't tolerate any of that crap. I recognize what the corruption is in the United States; I recognize the weak-kneed character of our leading politicians. That doesn't mean that they're bad people by intention. It means that they use the phrase, "You have to be practical." And when somebody says, as a candidate for something or other, or member of Congress, "You've got to be practical," I know they're not honest. They may wish to be honest; they may wish to do something good, but they tell you, that wouldn't be practical.

And therefore, the belief in practicality instead of

truth is the problem, and we've gotten to a point now, where the people of the United States, right now, based on what we can stimulate around the idea of Manhattan, around New York City—New York City is absolutely crucial to save the United States, it always was! This was defined very clearly by Alexander Hamilton, and if you look at the Hamiltonian policy, as he laid it out, particularly his four principles of economy; the only thing that's ever done any good for the economy of the United States has been based on consistency with a Hamiltonian policy. And you can look that up in the four statements he made, and what he did.

That's why he was assassinated by the British Empire. Because he was a threat; he was a threat to the British Empire. And when he was murdered, we didn't have a decent President in the United States until President John Quincy Adams. So, that's been the history. Lincoln was another case. Franklin Roosevelt was a major case, who, mysteriously, those guys got pushed out of the way or assassinated, one way or the other.

And the problem has been that the people who have courage don't have enough courage in order to defend those Presidents or Presidential candidates who are qualified to lead the nation to its proper destiny. And it's the cowardice of the practical members of society who give in, and thus open the gates for the tyrannies of people like the Bushes.

I mean, the Bush family, that is the followers of Prescott Bush, the Hitler-backer! Prescott Bush. His family is the one that created the worst evil of the 20th Century, and yet people are still voting for Bushes. And I would say, Moses would say, "Burn the Bushes."

The Twentieth Century of Evil

Twelfth Question: Hi, this is J— from Minnesota. You touched on some of this—but more specifically, given the cohesion of the BRICS countries and their fi-

President Theodore Roosevelt's elevation to the Presidency in 1901 coincided with the downslide of American morals and culture.

nancial and economic development, including the banks, etc., are they as cohesive in their military backbone, as, say, Putin is, who is really getting the potshots aimed at him, given the ABM systems, and Poroshenko's threats. And just how close is Putin to telling these guys, "Enough is enough"?

LaRouche: OK. I think it's time to give you some bad news. But it's not necessarily bad news in the long run, because, accepting the fact that it is bad news, may prompt more people in the United States in particular, to recognize that they have to do something to change things. And the problem in the United States often is, that because of the educational system—. Let me break off there and come back to that.

The problem has been, that there was a turn in the history of civilization, which came at the point of the beginning of the 20th Century. The 20th Century was a period in which the moral and related qualities of the citizenry of the United States and in Europe generally, was degenerate, and has been increasingly degenerate ever since that time.

There have been fluctuations, like Franklin Roosevelt's Presidency, and a few other things, some of our other Presidents; a few other of our Presidents, who were good. I've worked with some Presidents who were good; they may not have been the best, but they were good. And I have worked with them. And I regret the fact that they were knocked out of control, and the Bushes were put in, instead. And mostly, the Bushes have been the problem. And I would say, that Moses would say, "Burn the Bushes." Get them out of the political system.

That's the problem. We are faced with the fact that the government of the United States is mismanaged. And it's mismanaged because of opportunism and cowardice. But the more particular thing is that the idea, the principle that was set into place, with the beginning of the 20th Century; in that time, the United States and its people, its education, and its system, has been in a progress of generally steady rottenness. That is, the incompetence of the minds of our citizens—and I mean all layers of citizens—they are incompetent! They don't know they're incompetent. But they say, they've got to do it because it's necessary for their benefit to, go along, to get along.

That is, go along, to get along is the essential satanic principle. Go along, to get along. Instead of going along, you have to respond to what you can understand to be the necessary laws, the necessary policies of nations and of ourselves, in particular. The corruption of our nation is terrible. And it's been increasing ever since, recently. Since the first Bushes were brought into the Presidency: the children and grandchildren of Prescott Bush, the Hitler-backer, who was the grandfather, shall we say, of the Bush family, politically. And that's where the problem is.

And the need is to understand what we must eliminate from this legacy, because there have been very few Presidents who were qualified actually to be entrusted with the Presidency. Very few. And that's been the legacy.

And the British Empire has been, chiefly, the agency which has maintained that policy. The attempted assassination of Reagan, for example. The assassination of Presidents, were always done by the British Empire. Every assassination of a U.S. President was done by the British Empire. And yet, people sit and they ignore that, or they pretend to ignore it.

The question is, we have to build ourselves intellectually, into a body of people who understands what it must do to save this nation, and to realize the intention built into that nation. Very few Americans have any understanding of how the system works. They believe that you've got to be practical. Be practical. Be practical.

Well, being practical is being stupid. Because what you are doing, is that you are compromising what you should know—heh—in order to be accepted by society otherwise. The [lack of] guts to see the truth of a situation is a great weakness. And the incompetence of our educational system—don't kid yourself—the educational system of the United States, since the beginning of the 20th Century, has been a rotten education. And it's destroyed the ability of most citizens of the United States to be able to think clearly.

And that's what you've got to really work on.

Thirteenth Question: in California. First, I've got to say, God bless you, Lyn, for everything that you're doing. I really appreciate it very much.

LaRouche: Thank you.

Q: I have a couple of concerns. Well, the other night, I didn't know whether or not we were going to be blown up, or whatever, because these Russian bombers were flying over the coast of California. And now, I understand that the Jade Helm is taking over Wal-Mart, and using the empty Wal-Marts to set up their FEMA camps and, they're looking to bring people like myself—and you know, I can't even leave the country, because I've got family over here. And they're looking to march us into these FEMA camps, and destroy us. And that was my major concern about that. Are they going to be able to do that now? Because they're setting up, right at this moment.

LaRouche: I know. They are. Exactly. The water issue is the key. And what Obama is doing, and what the governor of California is doing, unlike his father, who was a decent man, and a good man. He may have had faults, but he was a good man. The son is no damn good at all. And has a record of being no damn good. And that's an ugly fact.

And the weakness, you see, all of California has degenerated. And the water crisis in California, is an example of, a product of, the kind of administration which California in particular has undergone under recent heads of government in California. I mean, some of the people they have brought in as governors in California were the worst monsters on the planet! Some of them were actually Nazis, who became the governors of California! A real Nazi, who had all kinds of sexual peculiarities, and was also a movie star. And he did all kinds of evil things on the screen.

So we have this problem. Only you can deal with this problem: you've got to fight the evil. And that's what I do.

Now fighting the evil is not always a successful venture as such. But it's like putting out forest fires. You may not be successful in stopping the forest fire, but you've got to take everything you can do, and fight against the forest fire. And that's what we've got to do. You've got to have your courage. And you've got to have a sense of solidarity, with not only our own nation and people, but also with other nations, which have honest concerns. They may not always agree on what

Press Information Bureau of India

Indian Prime Minister Narendra Modi on his May 15 visit to Beijing.

they think the solution is, but at least, they have the *intention* of solving the problem.

We have a situation now, which is very promising. China is the leading power in terms of economics and rates of progress in the entire world. China is presently, under this new regime in China—China always had some of these elements in it—but you also had bad administrations. But China now is the leading nation on the planet. That is, leading in terms of morally, in terms of rates of progress, and so forth. And all the problems they have, are simply things which can be easily understood.

India, which is practically following on the heels of what China is doing, typifies the process. Also, in certain parts of South America, you're finding optimistic trends in that part of the world, and options in that part of the world.

So, what we have to do, is that you have to work from a positive standpoint, of trying to get solidarity with forces in the world who represent the positive viewpoint, apart from what Europe—Europe in general—is a disaster. Why? Because it's just capitulated to the British Empire. The British Empire has poisoned, actually poisoned Europe.

In Russia, forces have come out of this same process, and Russia is now a power. A major power. And China is a major power of the planet. A leading nation of the planet. India—a major nation of the planet. Egypt

has come to a revival, a very promising revival. And things like that.

So, we have to actually always go—it's like fighting a war. And, I've had some experience with that. I was not out there shooting people. I've also been involved in fighting wars; and I put a lot of risk to myself, in fighting wars.

We are fighters against this crap. And we're not enough of us. So I would hope to increase the number of people who are inclined under these present circumstances, to realize that we have to fight. You can't sit back and put the blame. You've got to find out some way—either you fight, or you find some friends of yours who'll come out and do the leading and the fighting. That's the secret of this whole thing. Inspire your neighbors.

Ascher: I think that's a tremendous challenge for everybody on the call here this evening, Lyn… How long do you want to go, Lyn?

LaRouche: OK. As long as I—until I faint!

What's Happened to the American People?

Fourteenth Question: Hello, Lyn. I'm from Seattle, and I'm starting a relationship with a young German woman—can you give me any advice? [laughter]

LaRouche: I would say you have to cultivate your insight into your options. I wouldn't want to make any blanket statement on that subject. I think some of the ladies of Germany also have worries, so we don't have to put it on the other side only. They also have worries.

What we have to do is, we have to make nations which are now frightened, or which feel that they have to follow a track of corruption, or opportunism, as it's called, and they don't have the guts to stand up before what they should know is right. They say, "Well, I know that some people think this is right, but look, I'm a poor person. You've got to give me some breaks here. I can't do good things. I have to somehow, if I have to cheat a little bit, I'm going to cheat. Because I have to take care of *me!*"

So, their sense of social outlook is rather impaired, and it's not really all their fault. You look at the conditions of life in most parts of Europe. Look at Spain. Look at Portugal. Look at Italy. Look at much of the conditions in France. Look at the conditions in many parts of Germany. Look at what's happening to the Greeks. Look at these issues—and obviously, these nations are terrified. They're crushed. And the opportun-

opisfoundation.org

"What has happened to our people?"

ists are trying to parasitize their own neighbors and friends.

What we have to do is, we have to be a moral force, an influence, from among nations and groups of people who really understand that we have to fight, to get rid of the British Empire, to shut down the Saudi Empire—which is nothing but an extension of the British Empire—and other kinds of scoundrels. We have some of the most evil, most clear satanic people on the planet, which are centered in whole areas of the world, which used to have people who were not necessarily in the best condition, but at least had some sense of moral quality, in their idea about the nature of mankind.

What you're seeing now, in the Middle East, you're seeing the most horrible kind of genocide; it's spreading throughout this whole region. What Obama did, in North Africa—Obama's one of the most satanic, evil persons on this planet. That's a fact!

And so therefore, the poor guy out there, who's the ordinary citizen of some nation or another nation, what is this person able to do, to fight against the evil represented by Saudi Arabia—which is nothing but a tool of the British Empire? They're evil, absolutely evil.

And the President of the United States is absolutely evil—Obama. He's systemically evil. And he was put in power by the British Empire. And I could give you, if you wanted to go through it, the names of the people who did that.

So, the problem is, we need people with the guts,

and also the mental temperament and knowledge, to lead our people, to resist this kind of corruption, which has brought us to the system we're in right today.

Look at the condition of the American citizen! Look at our citizens! What's happened to them? What's happened to our citizens? What's their standard of living, the typical citizen? Where's the employment? Where's the education? How many are drug addicts? How many are destroyed in one way or another?

How about all the black citizens of the United States, in the southern region, who, like the case in the center of the area? They don't have a chance. They once had the area in which there was great production, great productive capabilities, economic progress—and it's all garbage now. It's destroyed. It's destroyed by the Bush family. The Bush family is the instrument which has led in destroying the economy of the United States. And Prescott Bush was never any damn good.

Fifteenth Question: Hi, I'm from Texas. The question I wanted to ask—this ionization, is it active? I mean, are they using this anywhere around Texas? … We're getting flooded out. I'm just wondering if they are tapping those rivers now. Texas is real big on privatization—and I know there are private companies that do that.

LaRouche: Well, it's going into effect, but this is a complicated problem. It's a scientific effect, and it depends upon the width and depth of the implementation of the policy. What Ben has done, so far, is a revolution. It's a revolution that is necessary; it's a revolution which could save many parts of the nation. It could save California, from the destruction which is hitting it now. It could be done.

But the present governor of California will not let that happen. The present governor of California is prepared to commit genocide against the people of California—and don't kid yourself about that. That's what he is doing. This man is a genocidalist. And he doesn't belong in office.

And these are the kinds of problems we have to deal with. We have to actually fight the forces of evil, and I'm afraid the current governor of California, has manifested himself *explicitly*, out of his own mouth, as an agent of evil, on the water question—and other things. And the plan to commit genocide against people! The California governor has now committed a policy which is actually genocide against the people.

And do you want to let that happen? Do you want to let that go? Do you want to allow that to continue? You want to support it? You want to say, oh, yes, oh yes? Or do you want to say, this guy has to be thrown out of office.

"We're not backing up our competent teachers."

The Decline of U.S. Education

Sixteenth Question: I want to thank Mr. LaRouche for his presence on the call tonight, and I've been listening carefully to all of the answers, which are phenomenal, to the questions that are being asked. And, as a teacher, and a New Yorker, and part of the Manhattan Project, I have a question that deals with dealing with different organizations, and trying to organize the people within those organizations.

I'm a delegate to an organization that represents 3,000 other delegates, and then represents all of the teachers of New York City. The leadership of this organization, they steer clear of openly criticizing Obama. But then they introduce resolutions that they want teachers to support, that clearly show that they realize that their lives are going down the tubes.

So my question is, when they introduce these resolutions, like Workers' Rights, and single-payer health policies, and they want to defend Medicare and Social Security, and they want teachers to support the defense for the introduction of these things, what if they were questioned on not being sucked into these single issues, and showing the connection between all of these issues, and Glass-Steagall?

LaRouche: Okay, Glass-Steagall. Glass-Steagall is obviously a mandatory policy. Because the very idea of the education of the citizen to be functional, and to understand what the world is all about, at least to some degree, depends upon the Glass-Steagall principle. Which is the rights of the citizen to find out what the issue is.

Now, the educational process in the United States, since the Bush family moved into the presidency business, actively, has destroyed the ability of the citizenry. You can't teach it. You're not supposed to teach it. There are principles of education. We used to have them. They weren't perfect, but they represented the fact that some people in the teaching business were able to actually be the exceptions, to be the leaders of the progress of the education of our citizens.

That has been crushed. It's not allowed any more. It's cut off. And therefore, it's a fighting issue.

Now, Obama has been really a very bad factor in this thing. It's not just a New York issue—he's generally a universal idiot. He's really not an intelligent person. But he's an instrument of the British Empire. And he's created great crimes against the citizens of the United States, by intimidation. They're afraid of him. He's a very vicious man. He's evil.

But that's not the problem. How did he get put into power? He did not honestly earn his election. He was run from the British Empire. And you look at the last phase—you know, Hillary was not the greatest candidate that ever walked down the line, but she was precious, compared to Obama. Obama is evil, purely evil. He's a force of evil. He has no real competence, no real scientific competence, nothing significant. He's a fraud.

But he has a backing, and the backing comes from the British Queen, from the British power. So, he's a British stooge.

And this has happened before. We do not provide, since the 20th Century, the beginning of the 20th Century, we no longer provide for the kind of educational program which is needed, and which was understood up to the beginning of the last century. We've been going down hill.

And, you know, I have a fight against what I ran into in education in the 1920s, when I was born, and was crawling up into things, and I had a good experience in education, because I knew what was wrong with it. I caught onto that pretty well. And we've done a lot of good work in that. But the point is, I understand the problem. We are not providing, to the teachers, who have competence, who *had* competence—we're not backing them up any more. We are actually pulling them down. We're suppressing them. We're telling them to do this, give in, give in, give in.

And in New York City? Look, in New York City, if we had our druthers—because I know New York City pretty well—if we had our druthers, and we had some of the kinds of leaders in New York that we had earlier, who had some power and influence in New York City—none of this would have been allowed. None of this would ever have happened. The Franklin Roosevelt tradition was still a very powerful influence.

And what we can say, honestly, we must, and can, restore the kind of development of educational programs, for our students, for our children, which will enable them, equip them, to cope with the challenge of understanding science and human culture generally. And we have to do it. And we're going to have to make a fight about it. We're going to have to do it.

We do have to be careful, because we don't want to create unnecessary victims, because people will take it out on citizens if they can. But, in principle, we have to understand among ourselves, that we have the devotion, we have a mission, and for the teachers, or other professions of relevance, we're going to have to work with them, assist them, to help defend them in their endeavors to do the job they want to do.

Seventeenth Question: I'm C— from Philadelphia. You spoke to the issue of water being the problem to do away with the people in California and elsewhere. There is another equally important issue that I think a lot of people may not be aware of, and we just have to look up. It's weather geo-engineering, or what some people call chem-trails. Can you address that, please?

LaRouche: What we have as the answer to that, is we have the galactic principle. Now, the galactic principle was not something which was discovered as such; it was not invented at some point. It was invented a very long time ago. But the galactic system is the system that enables us to develop the water system, which is necessary for human life, and for related things.

What has happened now, as in California, for example, their program is to *prevent* the development of the water program. We know, and we have experiments to show it, we have scientific principles which we know, galactic principles—and what the whole water system of the planet, planet Earth, is located in this location. And that's where the water comes from. It comes from the galaxy, not from Earth. Yes, there's water on earth. But the main stock of water for mankind, comes from the galaxy, from the context of the galaxy.

Now, this is well known among scientists, but it's denied by politicians, the current politicians. They're lying. There is no reason why we cannot introduce a water reform, which is based on galactic considerations, and to use the technologies which the study of the galactic process—Remember, the water system of Planet Earth is located in the galaxy, the dominant part of that. Located there. The question of managing life on Earth, often involves the management, the ability to manage, the galactic process.

Now that is manageable. There are ways you can get at the management. There are also policies by which we can improve water purification. Because it's not just the water; it has to be processed in a way in which it can do the job it has to do. So, there's no reason for allowing what is happening in California, in particular—and the adjacent areas—there is no reason for that to be allowed to continue. It only exists because of people like the governor of California, who is murdering the citizens of California.

Because the California crisis should not have developed, had the known science been applied to these questions. Now, the knowledge of these principles is limited. That's unfortunate. But the corrections could be made. The solutions can be found. The means exist, and close associates of mine are associated with this venture. So there's no excuse for accepting such a condition.

Destroy Wall Street

Eighteenth Question: I'm from New York City. It's a pleasure to finally speak with you, Lyn. My question, how can we the people convince our Assembly people to sign on the Glass-Steagall resolution, and how would that affect our fight?

LaRouche: My view is, you don't have to go out and use physical violence. But you do have to tell them—Well, take the Wall Street people: They're Wall Street people, generally—they're not really human. That is, they could be human. They have the biological potential of being human, but they have chosen to avoid that, the use of that mechanism. And they would like to have money instead.

The problem, of course, is, for Wall Street, the money of Wall Street is worthless, but people still worship it. Why do they worship it? Because it's something they don't know anything about. A typical kind of problem. I think we can try to educate some people on this.

But the real thing is, in New York City, in particular, which I know fairly well—I spent a lot of time in New York City in the course of my life. In New York City, we have a rich lode of ordinary citizens, who are probably a little more old nowadays, teachers and so forth, who know about these things. We have a force in New York City areas, where we have some of the smartest people in the United States, in terms of ordinary citizens. You used to have that around Boston. Boston has lost some of its brains under recent management.

EIRNS/Stuart Lewis
Alexander Hamilton's statue in Manhattan

But New York City is really still the center of thinking of the United States, because it's the Alexander Hamilton symptom. Now there were other people who made our nation as a nation, but Alexander Hamilton was the crucial figure, and he was assassinated by the British, for that reason. But Alexander Hamilton set forth a policy, an economic policy. That economic policy is the only policy which has ever been suitable to the requirements of the people of the United States.

That policy has been increasingly destroyed—by the Confederacy, for example. Most of the Presidents of the 20th Century of the United States were incompetents, or maliciously incompetent. We had a few presidents who were actually competent, and represented what the United States represents. We had a concentration in New York City, in particular, among young people who had a decent education in those times—they were not always the richest part of the population, but they were intelligent people, and they absorbed things. They had the ambition of being successful, in terms of family life, in terms of the outcome of family life within the family itself.

That was somewhat depressed. But it's still in effect. New York City is the intellectual center of the United States. And that's a fact. You have other parts of the United States which share the same talent that New York City represents at its best, but New York City itself—Boston used to be an important area: it's run down considerably since that time. But the point is, the situation in New York City is the intellectual center of the United States.

And we have to understand that those citizens, who may not been the richest citizens in the whole place, but who have a family tradition, a devotion to success. We have immigrants who come in from different parts of the world into the United States, or around it, and they share that. So, even though they're not the richest people in the world—which is not really, necessarily a necessity—but the fact is that we have citizens who have come to reside in New York City, the immigrants from various parts of the world, and they represent a family, a group of people... Probably—I don't know the exact percentage—but I would say a very large minority of the citizenry of New York City has this kind of special character, which is to be admired, as a model in the United States.

And I would to say that the best way to look at it, is to look at the achievements of Alexander Hamilton. He was the one who created the economic system of the United States. Made it work. Designed the principles.

Destroy Evil With Good

Nineteenth Question: This is A— from Columbia, Maryland. In view of the oil spill in California, what is your view of the environmental issues that we see in the United States?

LaRouche: It's terrible. The policy of the United States is awful. It's evil.

What they're doing, for example, in California—they're doing this mining [fracking] operation, so-called. And what they're doing is they're destroying the ability to maintain progress, physical progress, in California. And this is done by the "crackers" who have these projects. And they are destroying the resources of California itself. They're ruining the nation, that region.

And the same thing is going on in Texas. Texas is being destroyed by the mining operations, reckless operations. What happened with the British operation [BP oil spill] in the Gulf area, which destroyed a whole part of this function some years ago. And it was a British operation.

So this kind of operation is, should be outlawed, immediately outlawed. Because when you do mining which destroys to maintain the productivity of a part of the territory of the United States, and that does it maliciously and unnecessarily, it's a crime. And the guys should be in the jug. They should be in prison for a while, and caused to reflect upon their errors and their ways.

Twentieth Question: I'd like to thank you for conceiving of this organization, several times, considering generations of it, and conceiving of the IDB, which is now being created, conceiving of the *EIR*, conceiving of the Beam Defense Weapon, and many other beautiful conceptions that you've given us, including the collaboration with people like Helga. And I'd like to ask you, how did you first find out about Vernadsky's works, since he's been suppressed—you can hardly find anything about it in our history, just as Leibniz was suppressed in his age. And finally, what's the best way to deal with somebody who says, don't use the word evil, you can't use that word.

LaRouche: [laughs] Hitler was evil, don't you know? The British monarchy is evil. You've got to talk about evil. That's the most important subject to discuss on any occasion. The force of evil. If you look at the

EIRNS/Sylvia Spaniolo

Kesha Rogers' Texas Senate campaign in the town of Harlingen, January 2014.

history of the presidents of the United States, you find that, in the main, the history of the presidents of the United States are mostly evil, regrettable creatures who should not have been allowed to slither around the territory.

That's the point: you have to fight to maintain what is good. And what is good is not somebody's opinion: it's a question of—look, mankind is precious creature. There's nothing known in the universe which is a possible, plausible replacement for mankind. Mankind is God's own choice. That's the simple way to put it. And the powers that mankind has, the noetic powers, the ability to create new things, to create the existence of new forms of things in the universe—is specific to mankind. We don't *know* of any other source which can do that.

And therefore our main problem, and our main responsibility, is *we*, especially those of us who have the privilege of understanding science, and what science means in terms of practice, we have the responsibility, as leaders, in education, and related things—we have the responsibility of informing children growing up, adults, and so forth—and giving them the insight into what mankind really is. What mankind can be. And we have to know that, and that knowledge, and that outlook. We have to know what great art is, why the common art is such trash.

But the things that we could know, that we sometimes had known, as mankind—these things must be understood, located, and supported.

We need an educational program in that sense, which enables the average citizen to have access to the understanding of man's power to develop the universe, at least the nearby part, the galactic part.

Twenty-First Question: Hi, this is P— from Connecticut. Thank you, Mr. LaRouche, for being on the call. I recently had a great opportunity to unite the small and large businesses in Connecticut. The Governor of Connecticut proposed a $2 billion tax increase; they had public hearing on May 11th, in Hartford, and over 1,000 people showed up for it from all over the state. And after they testified, I spoke with them, and they were just livid, because this would put businesses out, small and large, and also jobs would be terminated.

So my plan is to unite the majority of the people to up-rise and join the LaRouche movement for peace, and give us the overwhelming unity for the American spirit.

LaRouche: Okay. There is a very simple response to that, simple in the sense, it's neat. Not simplistic, but neat.

The point is, we live in a system which is really dominated by the influence of the British system, the British Empire. And what we had as the American System, has been diluted. The Bushes, for example, the Bush family, starting with that old criminal, that pro-Nazi criminal, Prescott Bush! And the whole Bush family is a tribe of some kind of wild savages, which shouldn't be allowed into politics.

And so, this influence, and the influence of Wall Street, which is the same thing—what we have to do, is we have to shut down Wall Street! Look, Wall Street is totally useless, it's worse than useless, it's destroying the United States. It's destroying the citizens of the United States. It's destroying their families, destroying everything, destroying education, destroying science, everything!

So, what we have to do, is get rid of those kinds of people, in the sense of putting them out of business: we have to shut down Wall Street. Wall Street must be obliterated! We must go back to Glass-Steagall.

There's a very simple thing: If Glass-Steagall had not been repealed, we wouldn't have the mess we have today in the United States. So we've got to go back to Glass-Steagall; we've got to go back to that kind of condition. And that may not be an adequate measure, but it certainly is one of the measures which is essential to be contributing to the future of the United States.

The health care of the United States, the health care of our citizens! It's a crime! The way the health care is delivered is a crime! It's not done by the doctors, it's imposed upon the doctors. And the quality of medicine in terms of the standard of practice of medicine, is being destroyed! Or, it's so costly, most people can't get help.

The education system is so corrupt, so rotten, that the student in schools doesn't actually get any useful information. So we have come to the point, that we can even do these very simple things, on the scale of comparisons and say that we've been cheated, and we've been cheated, well, especially since about the 1980— since about that time. And we had Bill Clinton was actually a pretty good President; we may have criticized him on a number of things, but I know him, personally, well, and he's a pretty good guy. And he was one of the better Presidents we've had in the crop recently.

So, if we get back to some of those things which had been useful to the citizens of the United States, restore that, we would be moving on the way back up to what we had sought to do beforehand. And we can do it now.

But what we have to do, is mobilize our citizens who have the courage to recognize what their rights really are, what they have a right to demand, really should be. And we have to get rid of Wall Street, we have to get rid of what it represents; we have to get rid of the Bushes. As Moses would say, "Burn the Bushes," especially Prescott Bush. And all the crooks which have taken over the United States. And all the Presidents which should never have been elected. Because the best Presidents have always been assassinated—the usual routine of the British Empire.

So, that's what—we have the means, if we have the insight and the courage to see the insight that we should recognize, we can assemble ourselves around that cause, we can win. Doesn't mean it's guaranteed to us, but we have a chance of winning, and the chance of winning is the thing that's most worth doing.

Letter to the Editors

Having recently read in the "Galactic Man" issue of *EIR*, your report on "Albert Einstein's God," I recalled some of what I had read of Einstein's writings on this very subject. I began to think more on what I knew of Einstein's great discoveries, and, within that context, Lyndon LaRouche's constant and necessary warnings, against mathematics as the foundation for physics. From my earliest memories, it is poetry which has been, as the German poet Heinrich Heine said, "a holy plaything to me." And physics? Something to be shunned at all costs. But, when I read one of the greatest early essays of the economist LaRouche, "Poetry Must Begin To Supersede Mathematics in Physics,"[1] I thought a possible new world of play had emerged. It is those memories that have compelled me to write you.

In this essay, Mr. LaRouche boldly asserts:

Johann Wolfgang von Goethe

> *Poetry, and forms of music, painting, and sculpture ordered according to Neoplatonic poetic principles, serve as part of the essential training of the mind to master preconscious processes. In turn, only those aspects of artistic effort that serve that notion of the poetic principle are to be regarded as art.*

I then began to struggle with some of the more popular writings of Einstein published for the informed layman, and then some of the works of the great 19th-Century German scientists such as Friedrich Gauss, Bernhard Riemann, and Georg Cantor. I searched for confirmation of their roots in poetry. And as I did, a slightly clearer idea began to emerge. But it was not until I read an essay by the great German poet Friedrich Schiller, "The Aesthetical Estimation of Magnitude,"[2] that a clear and wonderful picture emerged.

I will not attempt to provide a detailed history of the relationship between the breakthroughs of German science in the latter half of the 19th Century, and the works of German poets such as Schiller and Johann Wolfgang Goethe, etc. But I thought I might be able to provide a few relevant quotes and references that might encourage many of your readers to investigate these areas on their own. I do wish to give some indication of how poetry has been absolutely essential in developing these ideas.

'Einstein was a man of the book...'

These are words of German-born American physicist Gerald Holton, after exhaustively reviewing, in 2008, the contents of Einstein's personal library at Princeton:

> Throughout his life, Einstein was a man of the book, to a much higher degree than most other scientists. The remarkably diverse collection of volumes in his library grew constantly. If we look only at the German-language books published before 1910 that survived Einstein's Princeton household, the list includes much of the canon of the time: Boltzmann, Buchner, Friedrich Hebbel, the works of Heine in two editions, Helmholtz, von Humboldt, the many books of Kant, Gotthold Lessing, Mach, Nietzsche, and Schopenhauer. But what loom largest are the collected works of Johann von Goethe in a 36-volume edition and another of 12 volumes, plus two volumes on his Optics [*Zur Farbenlehre*, 1810—ed.], and the exchange of letters between Goethe and Friedrich Schiller.

As a young boy, educated in the tradition of German public school education, Einstein was building a foun-

---

1. *Fusion*, October 1978.

2. See translation on the Schiller website

Friedrich Schiller, 1791 portrait by Anton Graff

uplifting of mind, character, and spirit that characterized the rising portion of the *Bürgertum* [middle class-ed.]. This was especially true for its Jewish segments. *Kultur* advocated and legitimized emancipation, and also provided a vehicle of social assimilation.

After providing a brief history of Einstein's youth and education, Holton concludes with the following summation:

After all, during his scientifically most creative and intense period in Bern, Einstein formed with two young friends an academy for the self-study of scientific, philosophical, and literary classics. We have the list of the books they read and discussed at their meetings, which sometimes convened several times a week: Spinoza, Hume, Mach, Avenarius, Karl Pearson, Ampère, Helmholtz, Riemann, Dedekind, Clifford, Poincaré, John Stuart Mill, and Kirchhoff, as well as Sophocles and Racine, Cervantes and Dickens. They would not have wanted to be ignorant of the cultural milieu, even if they did not necessarily agree with all they read.

dation upon which the edifice of his genius could be raised. In *Dædalus, the Journal of the American Academy of Arts and Sciences*, in another essay on Einstein entitled, "The Roots of Science in the Cultural Soil," Holton elaborates on the foundations of Einstein's education:

Other points pale in comparison to a central one: Einstein's lifelong interest in and devotion to the European literary and philosophical cultural tradition, and especially to German literary and philosophical *Kultur*. That allegiance, in which his science was clearly embedded, had been fostered early in his childhood. While the classics of music were offered in their home by his mother, Einstein's father would assemble the family in the evening around the lamplight to read aloud from works by such writers as Friedrich Schiller or Heinrich Heine. The family perceived itself as participating in the movement of general *Bildung* in this way, the

Relativity: The Special and General Theory

Relativity: The Special and General Theory, is Einstein's own popular translation of the physics that shaped our truths of space and time. From the beginning he challenges all the contemporary assumptions of mathematics and physics. He demonstrates that physics must be grounded not only in the science of Ampère, Helmholtz, and Riemann, but also in the *Kultur* of the classics created by men like Beethoven and Schiller.

In Einstein's works for the layman, we see echoes of Schiller's writings, especially the "Aesthetical Estimation of Magnitude," where Schiller provides the necessary aesthetic foundation for the later works of Riemann and, eventually, Einstein. But before we approach Schiller, we must look briefly at Riemann's "Habilitation Dissertation," an elaboration of one of the greatest analyses of the relation between mathematics and physics, establishing the axioms of new,

Bernhard Riemann

more appropriate geometry.[3]

Riemann begins his dissertation by establishing a foundation for the actual measurement of space and time. Though this introduction is straightforward, it is not an easy read. Yet, it is certainly comprehensible for the informed layman willing to take the time and effort to study it. Riemann introduces his dissertation with a simple statement:

It is known that geometry assumes both the notion of space and the first principles of constructions in space, as given in advance. She gives definitions of them which are merely nominal, while the true determinations appear in the form of axioms. The relation of these assumptions remains consequently in darkness; we perceive neither whether nor how far their connection is necessary, nor, *a priori*, whether it is possible.

Riemann continues,

_____
3. This is a letter; it is meant to do nothing more or less than to interest the reader in investigating the connection among these three great geniuses of the 19th-Century renaissance of science.

From Euclid to Legendre (to name the most famous of modern reforming geometers) this darkness was cleared up neither by mathematicians nor by such philosophers as concerned themselves with it.

Riemann is emphasizing that geometrical notions of space and time, though empirically measurable, are nonetheless notions, hypotheses, assumptions, and are not themselves necessarily true. What we believe to be the causes of what we see, smell, and touch, so to speak, do not directly represent the causality behind these events, and therefore are not necessarily true. This is part of the foundation for the German scientific breakthroughs of 19th Century. And that foundation was, in great part, begun by the poet Schiller.

This is also the point that Einstein emphasizes: Mathematics is not science. It is merely a complex ruler, a measuring rod that tells you little about the causes of that which you are attempting to measure. More than any other great scientist, except perhaps LaRouche, Einstein's ability to educate the informed layman is part of his genius. In an essay entitled "Geometry and Experience," Einstein emphasizes:

At this point an enigma presents itself, which in all ages has agitated inquiring minds. How can it be that mathematics, being after all a product of human thought which is independent of experience, is so admirably appropriate to the objects of reality? Is human reason, then, without experience, merely by taking thought, able to fathom the properties of real things?

In my opinion, the answer to this question is, briefly, this: *As far as the propositions of mathematics refer to reality, they are not certain; and as far as they are certain, they do not refer to reality.* (emphasis added)

That is to say, mathematics tells us less and less about the nature of the physical world, to the extent to which we depend upon it to measure the physical world. Or to put it perhaps more simply: If it adds up perfectly, it tells us nothing about the nature of what we are counting.

'Aesthetical Estimation of Magnitude'

This notion as to an aethestic understanding of how we must investigate the relationship between Geometry and Experience, is admirably argued in Schiller's essay of 1793. This is the same great poet that Einstein's father would read to him and his siblings almost every evening as children. And I would find it difficult to believe that Einstein was unaware of this essay. Its significance lies in its opposition to those who denied any connection between beauty and the human creativity necessary for scientific advancement.

In this essay, Schiller demonstrates the essential idea that science must be grounded in an aesthetic appreciation of the universe. Science is not objective, nor is beauty somehow merely subjective, a matter of taste. It was Schiller who created the conceptual basis for those advances made in physics by Bernhard Riemann and Albert Einstein.

Schiller begins by asserting:

I can form four mental images, quite different from one another, of the quantity of an object. The tower which I see before me, is a magnitude.

It is 200 ells high.

It is high.

It is a high (sublime) object.

It is here that Schiller introduces a new axiom, for the foundations of a new geometry. The question of understanding any feature of the universe had to include "An Aesthetic Estimation of Magnitude," whether in physics, chemistry, or any feature of the physical sciences.

He concludes his essay with that same sense of aesthetics:

The highest mountain range is indeed small against the height of the firmament, but that is merely what the understanding teaches, not the eye, and it is not the heavens whose height makes the mountains low,—rather it is the mountains which, by their magnitude, show the elevation of the sky. It is, accordingly, not merely an *optically* correct, but also a *symbolically* true idea, when it is said, that Atlas holds up the heavens. Just as the heavens themselves literally seem to rest on Atlas, so our idea of the height of the heavens rests upon the height of Atlas. Thus the mountain, in the figurative sense, really holds up the heavens, because it holds the heavens aloft for our sensuous comprehension. Without the mountain, the heavens would fall, that is, they would sink before our eyes and be brought low (emphasis in original).

In this great, but little-read essay, Schiller is laying the foundation for what Einstein would later assert in his essay "The Religious Spirit of Science":

You will hardly find one among the profounder sort of scientific minds, without a religious feeling of his own. But it is different from the religiosity of the naïve man—the scientist is possessed by the sense of universal causation. The future, to him, is every whit as necessary and determined as the past.... His religious feeling takes the form of a rapturous amazement at the harmony of natural law, which reveals an intelligence of such superiority that, compared with it, all the systematic thinking and acting of human beings is an utterly insignificant reflection. This feeling is the guiding principle of his life and work....

Yours,
Theodore J. Andromidas

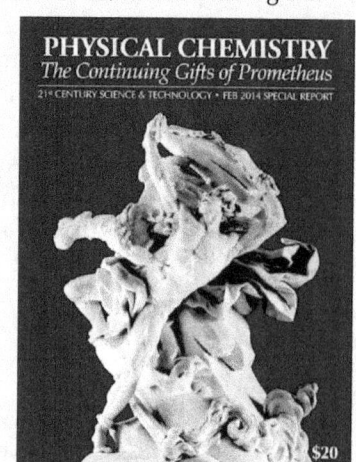